I0410906

United States
Department of
Agriculture

Forest
Service

Northern
Research Station

Resource Bulletin
NRS-21

PULPWOOD PRODUCTION IN THE NORTH-CENTRAL REGION, 2005

Ronald J. Piva

Abstract

Pulpwood production in the Lake States (Michigan, Minnesota, and Wisconsin) remained at 9.8 million cords in 2005, with 90 percent of that total from roundwood and 10 percent from the residue of wood-using mills. Aspen remained the dominant species harvested for pulpwood with 3.6 million cords or 40 percent of the total roundwood. From 2004 to 2005, softwood roundwood production increased by nearly 6 percent while hardwood roundwood production decreased by 1 percent. In 2005, 29 wood-pulp and 15 particleboard mills in the Lake States acquired 10.3 million cords of pulpwood, and increase of less than 1 percent from 2004. Pulpwood production in the Central States (Illinois, Indiana, Iowa, and Missouri) decreased by 2 percent, from 484 thousand cords in 2004 to 472 thousand cords in 2005. The Plains States (Kansas, Nebraska, North Dakota, South Dakota) produced 113 thousand cords of pulpwood from roundwood and mill residues, only 3 thousand fewer cords than in 2004.

The Author

RONALD J. PIVA is a forester with the Northern Research Station's Forest Inventory and Analysis Program.

CONTENTS

INTRODUCTION

Detailed information on pulpwood production[1] is needed for intelligent planning and decisionmaking in wood procurement, forest-resource management, forest-industry development, and scientific studies.

Primary products manufactured from reconstituted wood fiber include wood pulp, particleboard, and engineered lumber made from chips, shavings, wafers, flakes, strands, and sawdust. Reported here is the production of raw fiber material delivered to mills. These data reflect only that portion of the timber harvest used as raw material and not necessarily the volume of growing stock harvested.

Pulpwood constitutes more than half the industrial timber products harvested annually in the Lake States (Michigan, Minnesota, Wisconsin) and is an important product in the Central States (Illinois, Indiana, Iowa, Missouri) and Plains States (Kansas, Nebraska, North Dakota, South Dakota).

Since 1979, logs, bolts, and wood residue used in manufacturing flakeboard, waferboard, oriented strandboard (OSB), and medium-density fiberboard have been included in annual pulpwood reports. Engineered lumber was first included in 1992. Together, these products are called particleboard, and mills manufacturing these boards are referred to as particleboard mills in this report. Wood used at particleboard mills is identical or nearly identical to that used at pulp mills; therefore, including this wood in this report provides a more accurate estimate of demand for pulpwood-like material.

Particleboard mills were in their infancy before 1979 and used primarily aspen and wood residue. Therefore, data for these mills do not distort trends in roundwood use for other species or preclude comparing 2005 survey results with those of 1978 and previous years.

---

[1]Pulpwood production, determined from mill receipts, is the annual volume of pulpwood cut plus the annual wood-residue volume produced by sawmills, veneer mills, etc. for pulp, particleboard, waferboard, oriented strandboard, medium-density fiberboard, or engineered lumber.

Pulp and particleboard mills using timber from the North-Central region in 2005 reported their pulpwood receipts[2] by species group and county of origin. This report includes the results of the mill survey, compares results with those of 2004 and earlier years, and discusses trends in pulpwood production and use.

The Lake, Central, and Plains States are discussed separately because the timber types in each region differ and the flow of wood among regions is nominal. Results for pulpwood production and receipts are discussed at the broad regional level in the Central and Plains States to avoid revealing the operations of individual mills. This is the 47th annual report of the pulpwood harvest in Lake States counties, the 46th annual report of the Central States harvest, and the 13th report of the pulpwood harvest in the Plains States.

Several mills purchase their pulpwood based on weight rather than volume. Factors used to convert green tons of pulpwood to standard cord equivalents are shown in the Appendix.

When new surveys are completed, errors and omissions from previous surveys are corrected. As a result of ongoing efforts to improve the survey's efficiency and reliability, changes may have been made to the previous survey's data. All comparisons and analysis in this report are based on the reprocessed data from earlier surveys, which may not match earlier published data.

---

[2]Pulpwood receipts are the volumes of wood received by mills in a specific state or region, regardless of the geographic source.

LAKE STATES

PRODUCTION

- Pulpwood production in the Lake States remained at 9.8 million cords[3] in 2005. Ninety percent of this total was from roundwood (including chips from roundwood) and 10 percent was from the residue[4] of wood-using plants.

- In 2005, aspen remained the dominant species harvested for pulpwood in the Lake States with 3.6 million cords or 40 percent of the total roundwood. Other important species harvested for pulpwood in 2005 were soft maple (927 thousand cords), hard maple (916 thousand cords), white birch (634 thousand cords), and jack pine (543 thousand cords) (Fig. 1, Table 3).

- Softwood roundwood production increased by nearly 6 percent, from 1.7 million cords in 2004 to 1.8 million cords in 2005. Pulpwood production from softwood residues decreased by 7 percent to 476 thousand cords in 2005.

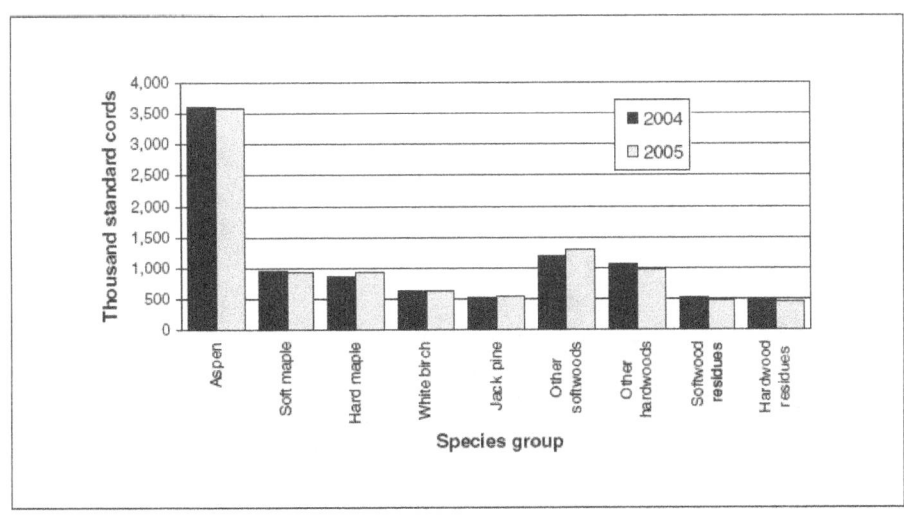

Figure 1.—Pulpwood production in the Lake States, by species group and residues, 2004-05.

---

[3]Refers to a standard cords, which is 128 cubic feet of wood, bark, and air space.
[4]Residue is the byproduct from sawmills, veneer mills, cooperage mills, and other wood-using mills that is used for pulping and particleboard. Residues include slabs, edgings, veneer cores, sawdust, fines, woodflour, and chips manufactured from slabs, edgings, and veneer cores.

- Hardwood roundwood production decreased by 1 percent, from 7.1 million cords in 2004 to 7.0 million cords in 2005. Hardwood residues decreased by nearly 4 percent during the same period.

Michigan

- Total production of pulpwood material in Michigan decreased by 6 percent, from 3.1 million cords in 2004 to 2.9 million cords in 2005. Pulpwood production from roundwood decreased by 4 percent while production from residues decreased by 17 percent (Fig. 2, Tables 4-5).

- In 2005, Northern Lower Peninsula and Western Upper Peninsula were the top pulpwood-producing Forest Inventory Units in the State with 972 thousand cords and 965 thousand cords harvested, respectively (Fig. 3, Tables 4-5).

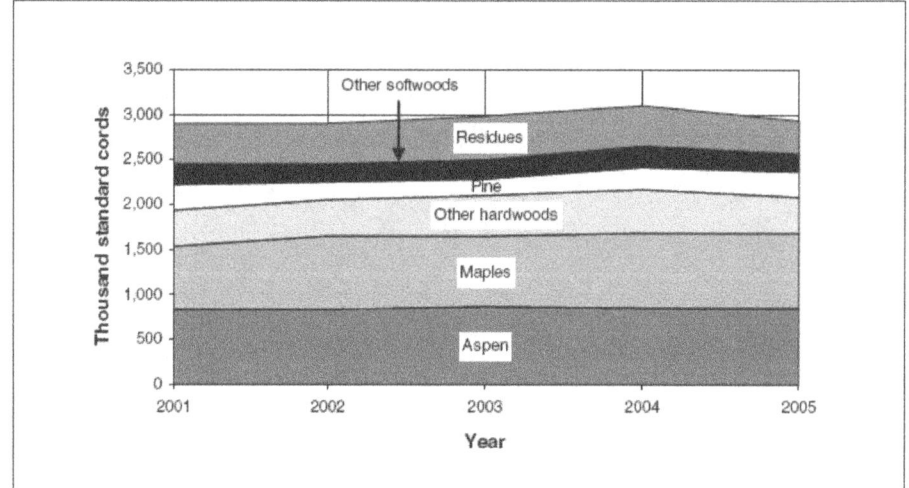

Figure 2.—Pulpwood production in Michigan, by species group and residues, 2001-05.

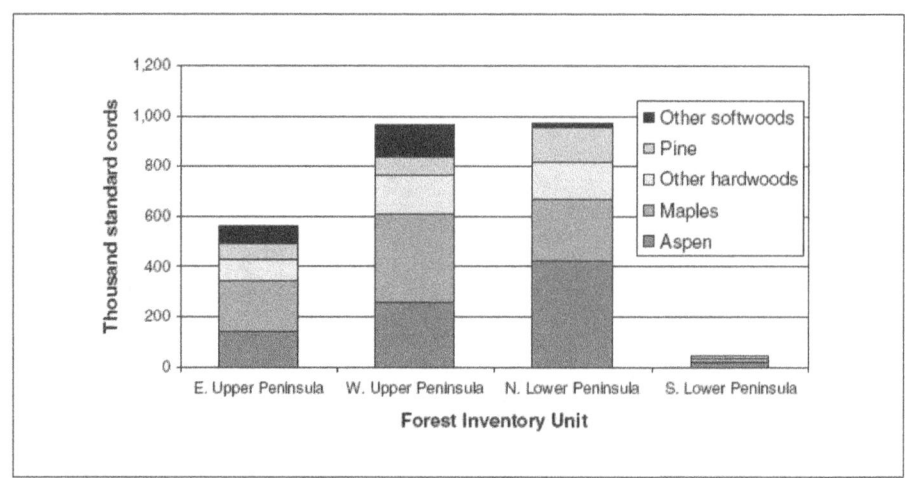

Figure 3.—Pulpwood production from roundwood in Michigan, by species group and Forest Inventory Unit, 2005.

4

Minnesota

- Between 2004 and 2005, Minnesota's total pulpwood production increased by 4 percent to 3.2 million cords. Roundwood pulpwood production increased by 5 percent and pulpwood produced from mill residues decreased by nearly 8 percent (Fig. 4).

- Aspen accounted for 60 percent of all the roundwood harvested for pulpwood in Minnesota in 2005.

- In 2005, the Northern Pine and Aspen-Birch Forest Inventory Units produced the most pulpwood from roundwood in the State, with 1.4 and 1.3 million cords of roundwood, respectively (Fig. 5, Table 8).

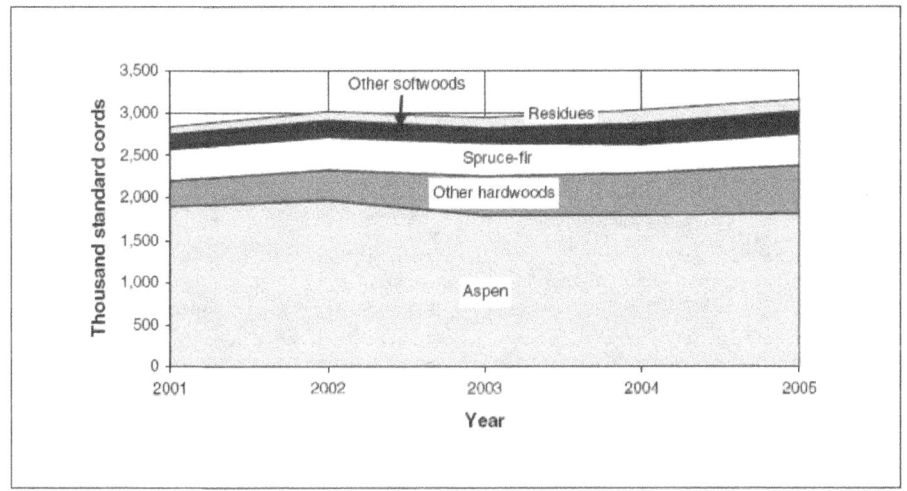

Figure 4.—Pulpwood production in Minnesota, by species group and residues, 2001-05.

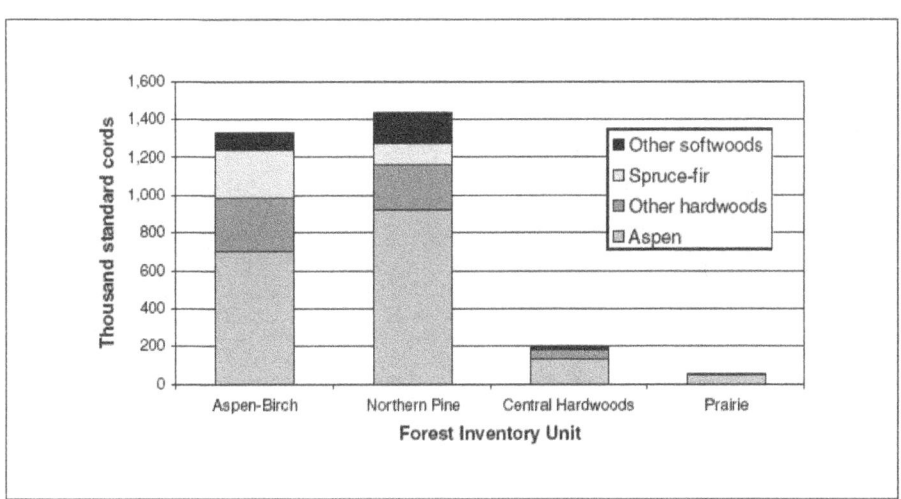

Figure 5.—Pulpwood production from roundwood in Minnesota, by species group and Forest Inventory Unit, 2005.

Wisconsin

- In 2005, pulpwood production in Wisconsin increased by fewer than 50 thousand cords, totaling 3.7 million cords. Pulpwood production from roundwood remained relatively unchanged while production from residues increased by 10 percent (Fig. 6).

- The Northwestern and Northeastern Forest Inventory Units remained the top producers of roundwood for pulping with 1.4 and 1.2 million cords, respectively (Fig. 7, Table 9).

Harvest Intensity

- In this report, the distribution of the harvest is shown in two ways. The amount of pulpwood cut relative to growing-stock volume for each of five major pulpwood species is shown in Figure 8. The amount of pulpwood relative to commercial timberland area is shown in Figure 9.

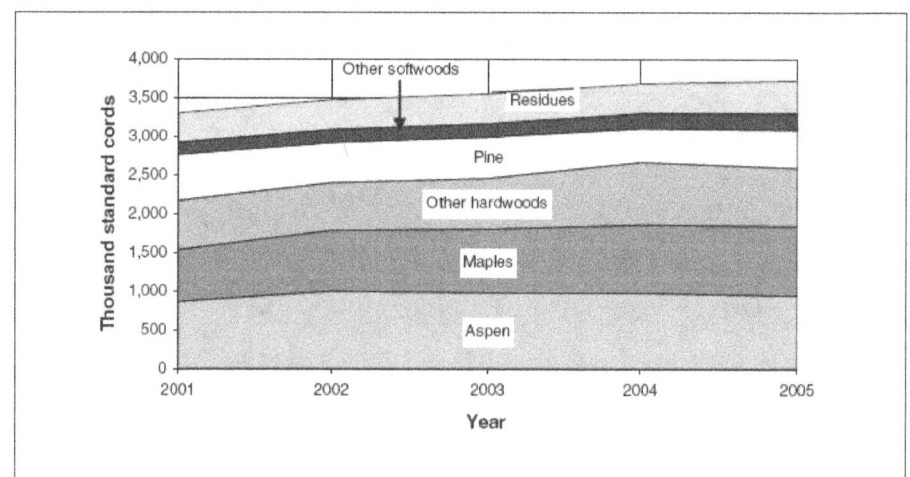

Figure 6.—Pulpwood production in Wisconsin, by species group and residues, 2001-05.

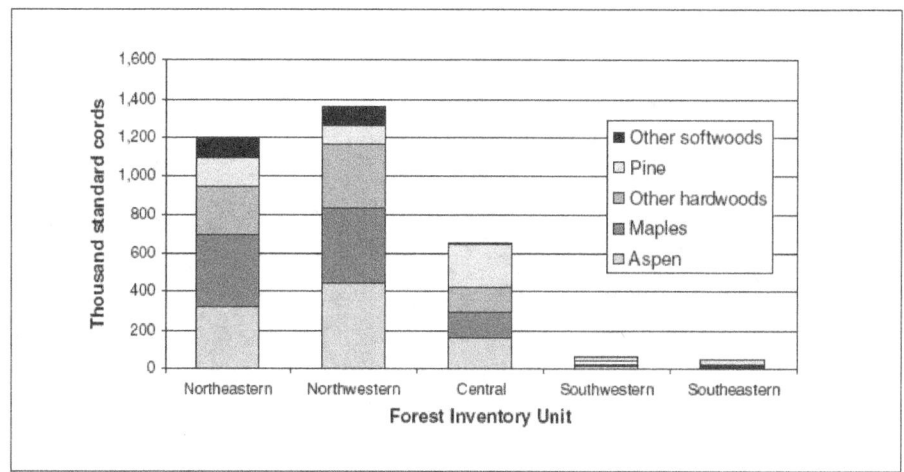

Figure 7.—Pulpwood production from roundwood in Wisconsin, by species group and Forest Inventory Unit, 2005.

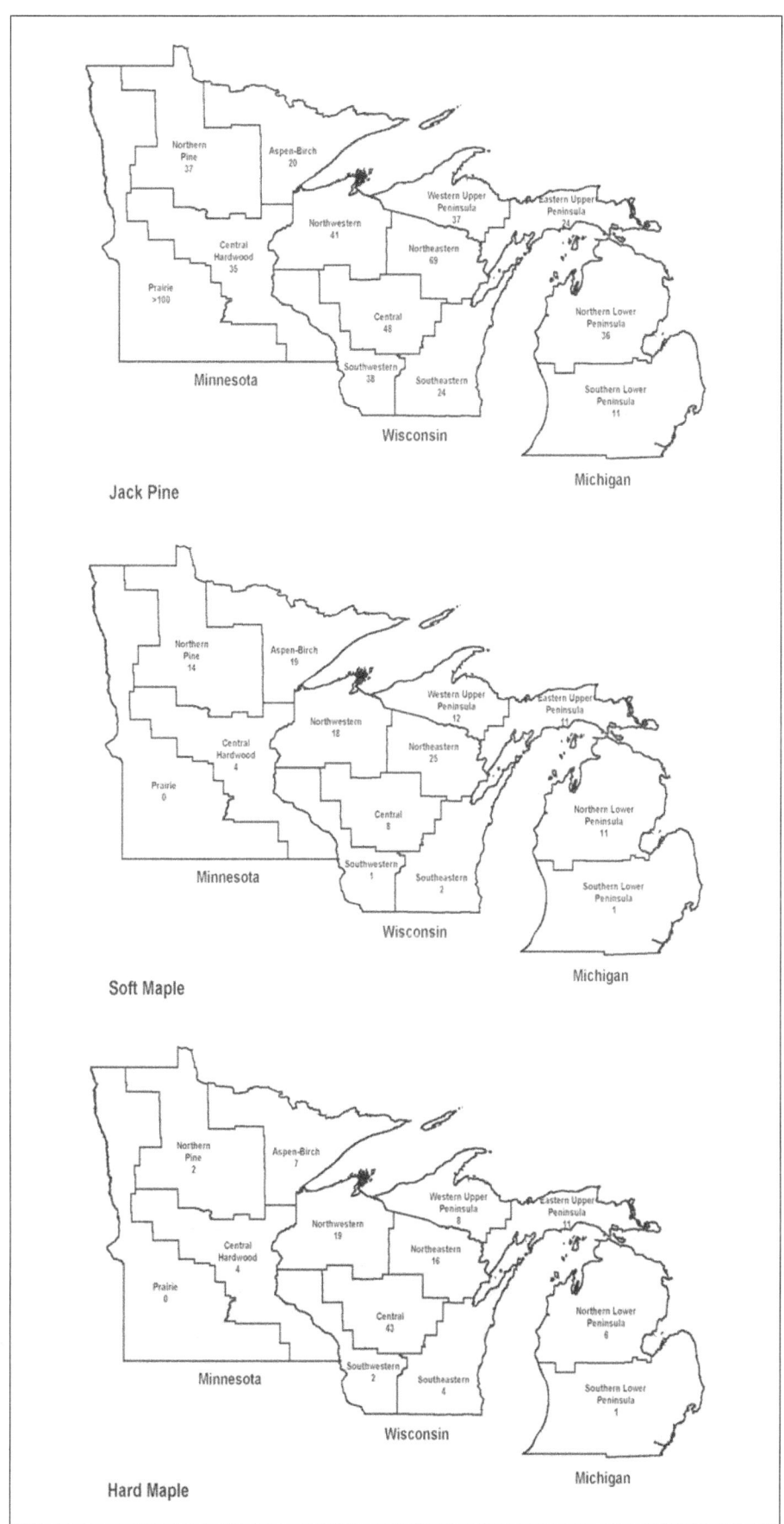

Jack Pine

Soft Maple

Hard Maple

Figure 8.—Cords of roundwood pulpwood (including chips from roundwood) harvested per 1,000 cords of growing-stock volume for each of five major pulpwood species, by state and Forest Inventory Unit, 2005.

(Figure 8 continued on next page)

(Figure 8 continued)

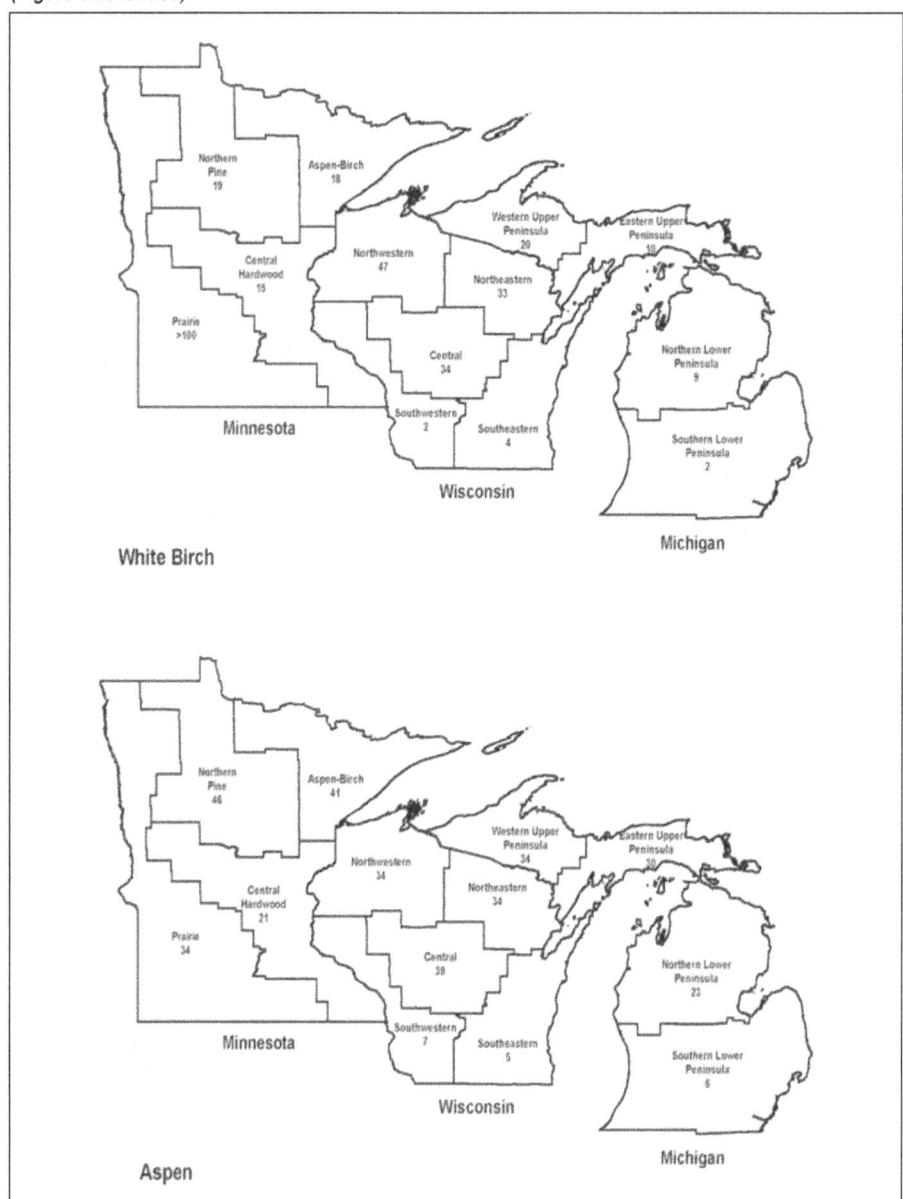

White Birch

Aspen

Figure 8. *(continued)*— Cords of roundwood pulpwood (including chips from roundwood) harvested per 1,000 cords of growing-stock volume for each of five major pulpwood species, by state and Forest Inventory Unit, 2005.

RECEIPTS

- In 2005, 29 wood pulp and 15 particleboard mills in the Lake States acquired 10.3 million cords of pulpwood, an increase of less than 1 percent from 2004.

- Aspen roundwood was processed at 35 of the 44 pulp and particleboard plants in 2005. Hardwood roundwood was processed at 41 of the plants in the Lake States (Table 10).

- In 2005, Wisconsin supplied wood to 36 mills, followed by Michigan (34), and Minnesota (26).

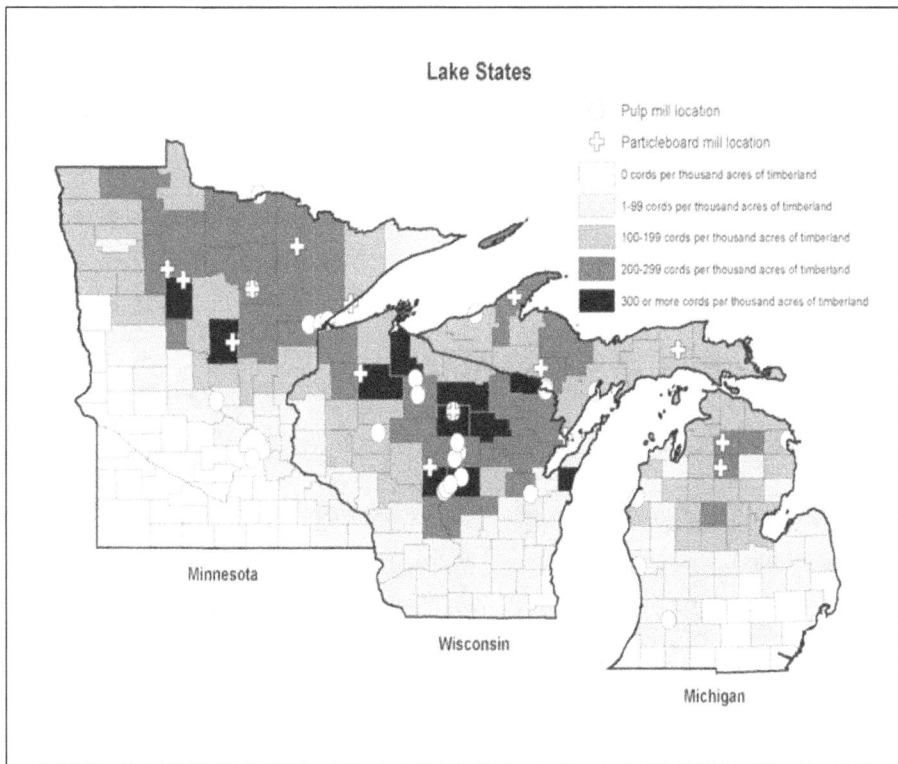

Figure 9.—Cords of pulpwood cut per thousand acres of timberland, by county, 2005. (Map shows active pulp and particleboard mills.)

- Imports of roundwood to Lake States pulp and particleboard mills increased by 10 percent and mill-residue imports increased by 80 percent between 2004 and 2005. Imports of all wood material in 2005 totaled 562 thousand cords, an increase of 16 percent from 2004. Canada contributed 87 percent of the total import receipts.

Michigan

- Total receipts of wood material representing the seven Michigan pulp mills, three OSB mills, one particleboard mill, and one molded strandwood mill decreased by 1 percent, or 46 thousand cords between 2004 and 2005. Nearly 16 percent of the total wood material consumed came from out of state. Wisconsin supplied more than 70 percent of the imported wood material.

Minnesota

- The eight pulp mills, five OSB mills, and one laminated structural lumber mill in Minnesota consumed 3.7 million cords in 2005, an increase of 5 percent from 2004. Pulp and particleboard mills in Minnesota acquired 19 percent of their raw material from out of state. Wisconsin supplied over half of the imported wood material.

9

Wisconsin

- The 14 pulp mills, 2 OSB mills, and 2 particleboard mills in Wisconsin consumed 3.5 million cords in 2005, a decrease of nearly 3 percent from 2004. Fifteen percent of the total receipts were imported. Of the total wood material imported, more than half was brought in from Michigan.

INDUSTRY TRENDS AND ANALYSIS

Pulp Mills

For this section, pulp-mill products include wood-fiber products such as paper, paperboard, hardboard, insulation board, and medium-density fiberboard. All of these products are manufactured from wood that has been reduced to individual fibers, small fiber bundles, or fiber parts that are subsequently formed into a mat. Wood material from the Lake States sent to mills in other states and Canada is included.

- Of the 9.8 million cords of pulpwood produced in the Lake States in 2005, 6.9 million cords (70 percent) were used for wood-pulp products; 88 percent of the wood material was from roundwood and 12 percent was from mill residues (Table 1).

- Principal species harvested for pulp in the Lake States in 2005 were aspen (1.5 million cords), hard maple (880 thousand cords), soft maple (796 thousand cords), and white birch (526 thousand cords) (Fig. 10).

Table 1.—Lake States pulpwood production for pulp mills, 2001-2005
(In standard cords, unpeeled).

Product form/ species group	Pulpwood production				
	2001	2002	2003	2004	2005
Roundwood					
Softwoods	1,658	1,500	1,480	1,391	1,470
Aspen	1,707	1,854	1,588	1,768	1,534
Other hardwoods	2,320	2,573	2,744	3,086	3,045
Residues	804	825	880	832	801
Total	6,488	6,753	6,693	7,077	6,858

Note: Columns may not add due to rounding.

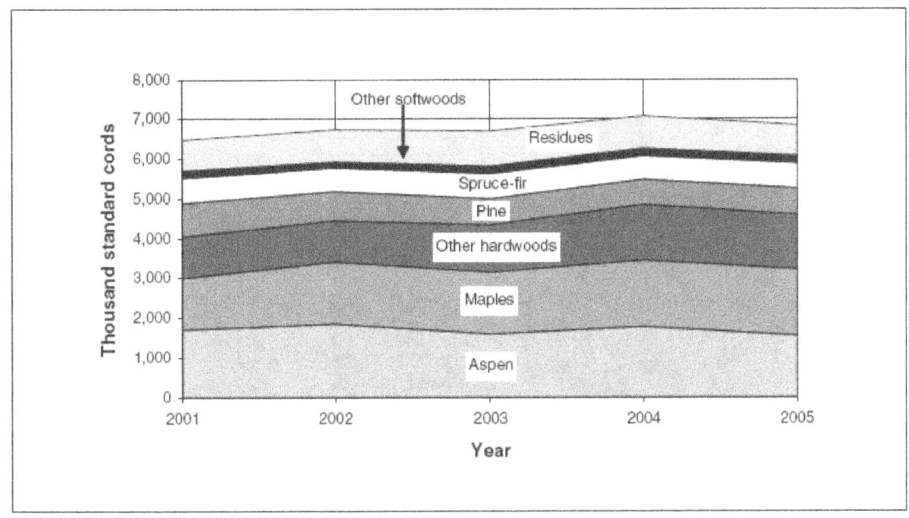

Figure 10.—Pulpwood production in the Lake States for pulp mills, by species group and residues, 2001-05.

- Hardwoods were the mainstay of the pulp mills in the Lake States in 2005. Hardwood roundwood contributed more than 67 percent of total raw material needs; hardwood residues supplied another 6 percent.

- Softwood roundwood harvested from the Lake States for pulp mills increased by nearly 6 percent between 2004 and 2005, while hardwood roundwood production decreased by 5 percent. Pulp mills used 4 percent less mill residues generated by primary wood-processing facilities in the Lake States in 2005 than in 2004.

- Average daily wood-pulp production decreased from 14.7 thousand tons of pulp per day in 2004 to 14.3 thousand tons of pulp per day in 2005 (Table 11).

Michigan

- Pulpwood production for wood pulp was 2.0 million cords in 2005, a decrease of nearly 9 percent from 2004 (Fig. 11).

- Soft maple, hard maple, and aspen were the major pulpwood species groups harvested in the State in 2005. Combined, these groups accounted for 60 percent of the total pulpwood harvested for wood-pulp production.

- Michigan wood-pulp mills imported 308 thousand cords of pulpwood, mostly from Wisconsin. Michigan exported about 346 thousand cords to wood-pulp mills in Minnesota, Wisconsin, and Canada.

11

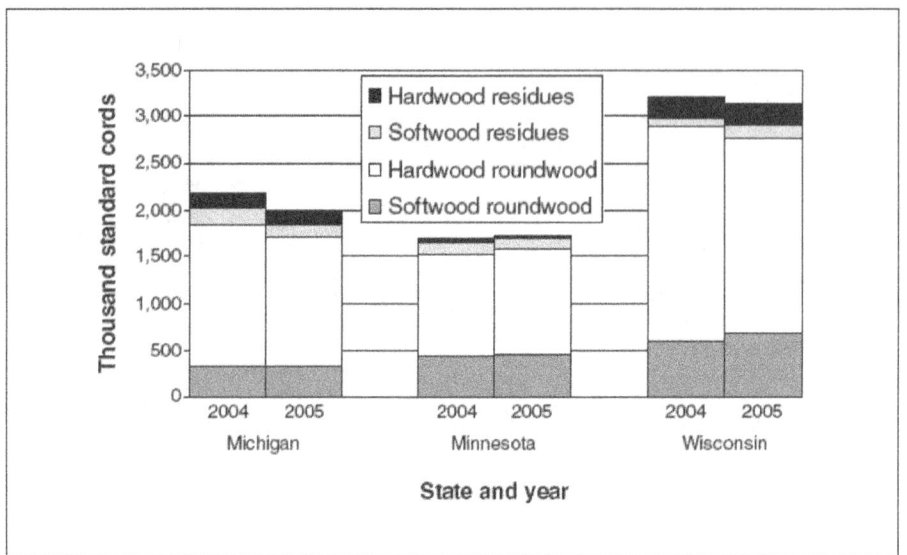

Figure 11.—Pulpwood production in the Lake States for pulp mills, by state, 2004-05.

Minnesota

- Pulpwood production for wood pulp totaled 1.7 million cords in 2005, an increase of 2 percent from 2004.

- In 2005, aspen remained the predominant species harvested in the State with 750 thousand cords or nearly half of the total roundwood produced. Other major species harvested were balsam fir (182 thousand cords), spruce (180 thousand cords), and white birch (164 thousand cords).

- Pulp mills in Minnesota imported 540 thousand cords of wood material from Michigan, North Dakota, Wisconsin, and Canada. Minnesota exported 129 thousand cords to pulp mills in Indiana, Wisconsin, and Canada.

Wisconsin

- Pulpwood production for wood pulp-products decreased by 2 percent to 3.1 million cords in 2005.

- Hard maple, aspen, and soft maple accounted for nearly half of the volume of roundwood harvested for pulp production.

- Wisconsin mills imported 461 thousand cords of pulpwood, with nearly 60 percent of the imports coming from Michigan. Wisconsin exported 367 thousand cords to Minnesota, 224 thousand cords to Michigan, and 21 thousand cords to other states.

Particleboard Mills

Particleboard is a generic term for a panel manufactured from lignocellulosic material—commonly wood—essentially in the form of particles (as distinct from fibers). These materials are bonded together with synthetic resin or other suitable binder under heat and pressure by a process wherein the interparticle bonds are created wholly by the added binder. Other materials may have been added during manufacture to improve certain properties. The many types of particleboard differ greatly in the size and geometry of the particle, the amount of resin (adhesive) used, and the density to which the panel is pressed. Products included in the particleboard group are particleboard, waferboard, OSB, and engineered lumber. The major types of particles used for particleboard are shavings, flakes, wafers, chips, sawdust, strands, slivers, and wood wool (excelsior). Much of the particleboard in the United States is made from residues (shavings, sawdust, or chips). Waferboard, OSB, and engineered lumber are examples of products requiring that the particles be cut from solid wood (saw logs or pulpwood). Wood material from the Lake States sent to mills in other states and Canada is included.

• In 2005, the Lake States produced nearly 3.0 million cords of pulpwood for particleboard products, an increase of about 8 percent from 2004 (Fig. 12).

• Eleven of the fifteen Lake States mills in the particleboard category were OSB or engineered-wood-product mills that require particles to be cut from roundwood. Hence, for every cord of pulpwood used in particleboard manufacture, 95 percent was from roundwood and 5 percent from residues.

• In 2005, aspen was the principal species harvested for particleboard products, accounting for 72 percent of the total roundwood harvested (Table 2).

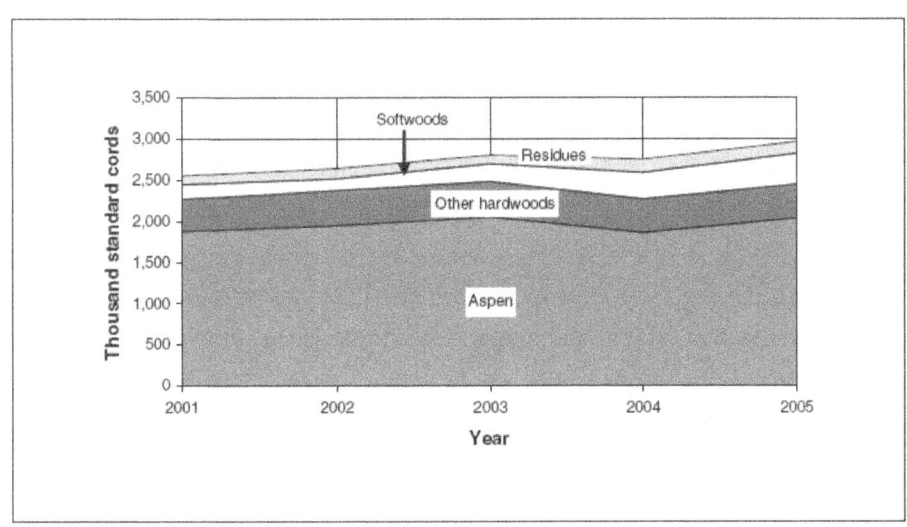

Figure 12.— Pulpwood production in the Lake States for particleboard mills, by species group and residues, 2001-05.

13

Table 2.—Lake States pulpwood production for particleboard mills, 2001-2005 (In standard cords, unpeeled).

Product form/ species group	Pulpwood production				
	2001	2002	2003	2004	2005
Roundwood					
Softwoods	174	149	204	316	368
Aspen	1,880	1,938	2,058	1,849	2,044
Other hardwoods	396	431	426	426	410
Residues	108	129	113	156	134
Total	2,558	2,647	2,801	2,747	2,957

Note: Columns may not add due to rounding.

- In 2005, the Lake States produced 368 thousand cords of softwood roundwood and 2.5 million cords of hardwood roundwood for processing at particleboard plants. All of the roundwood harvested in the Lake States for particleboard production was processed by mills in the Lake States.

- In 2005, the Lake States supplied 134 thousand cords of residues for use in particleboard production. Between 2004 and 2005, the use of residues for particleboard production decreased by 14 percent.

- Annual production at Lake States particleboard plants fell from 2,064 million square feet (¾-inch basis) in 2004 to 2,085 million square feet in 2005 (Table 12).

Michigan

- The production of wood material for particleboard production in Michigan rose from 918 thousand cords in 2004 to 924 thousand cords in 2005 (Fig. 13).

- In 2005, the harvest of roundwood from Michigan forest land provided 841 thousand cords of wood for particleboard products, of which more than 80 percent were hardwoods. Residues from Michigan's primary wood-using mills provided another 83 thousand cords of wood material used to produce particleboard products.

14

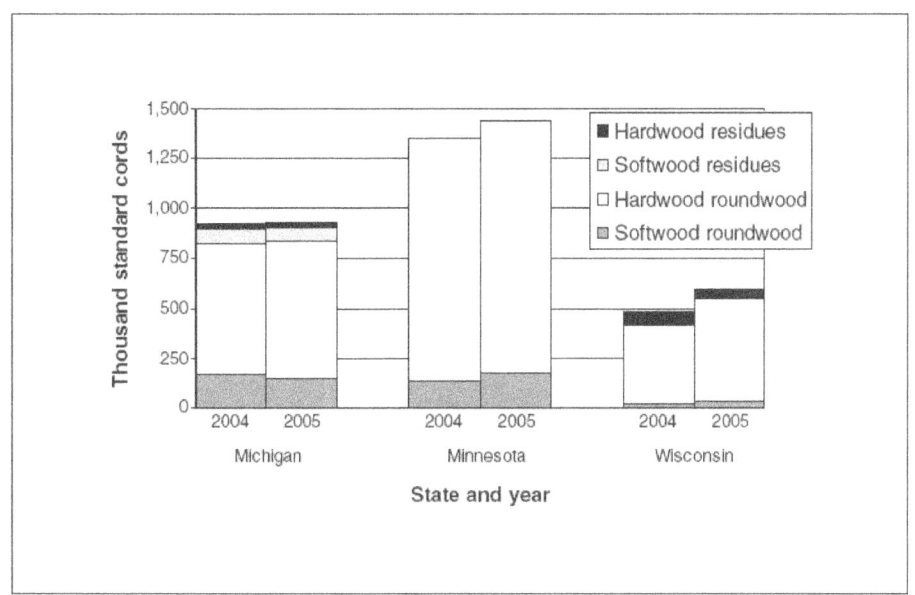

Figure 13.—Pulpwood production in the Lake States for particleboard mills, by state, 2004-05.

- The particleboard mills in Michigan imported 51 thousand cords from Canada and 110 thousand cords from Wisconsin. About 28 thousand cords of wood material for particleboard production were exported to Minnesota, Wisconsin, and Canada.

Minnesota

- The production of roundwood for particleboard production in Minnesota increased by 7 percent from 2004 to 2005, from 1.3 million cords in 2004 to 1.4 million cords in 2005. There were no residues from primary wood-using mills in Minnesota that were used in particleboard mills.

- In 2005, Minnesota accounted for nearly half of all the wood material produced in the Lake States for particleboard plants. Aspen remained the predominant species harvested (1.1 million cords) for particleboard production, accounting for about 75 percent of the total roundwood produced.

- The particleboard mills in Minnesota imported 154 thousand cords from Canada and 30 thousand cords from North Dakota, Wisconsin, and Michigan combined. In 2005, raw materials exported from the State for particleboard manufacturing totaled 38 thousand cords, all of which went to Wisconsin.

Wisconsin

- The production of wood material for particleboard production in Wisconsin increased by 24 percent, rising from 479 thousand cords in 2004 to 596 thousand cords in 2005.

- In 2005, 544 thousand cords of roundwood was harvested from Wisconsin forest land for the manufacturing of particleboard. The State's primary wood-processing mills provided an additional 51 thousand cords of plant byproducts to the particleboard industry.

- The mills in Wisconsin imported 80 thousand cords of wood for particleboard manufacturing: 75 thousand cords from Minnesota and Canada combined and 5 thousand cords from Michigan. Wisconsin exported 110 thousand cords to Michigan particleboard mills and 2 thousand cords to Minnesota particleboard mills.

CENTRAL STATES

PRODUCTION

Because of the limited number of pulp mills in the Central States, information by county is not reported to avoid disclosure of individual mill receipts.

- In 2005, pulpwood production in the Central States decreased by 2 percent, from 484 thousand cords in 2004 to 472 thousand cords.

- Pulpwood production from roundwood harvested in the Central States decreased by 19 percent, while pulpwood production from residues from primary wood-processing mills increased by 6 percent (Fig. 14).

- In 2005, wood residues accounted for about 72 percent of the total wood material produced in the Central States for the pulp and particleboard industry (Table 13).

- Production of softwood wood material increased by 40 thousand cords between 2004 and 2005, while production of hardwood wood material decreased by 52 thousand cords during the same period (Table 14).

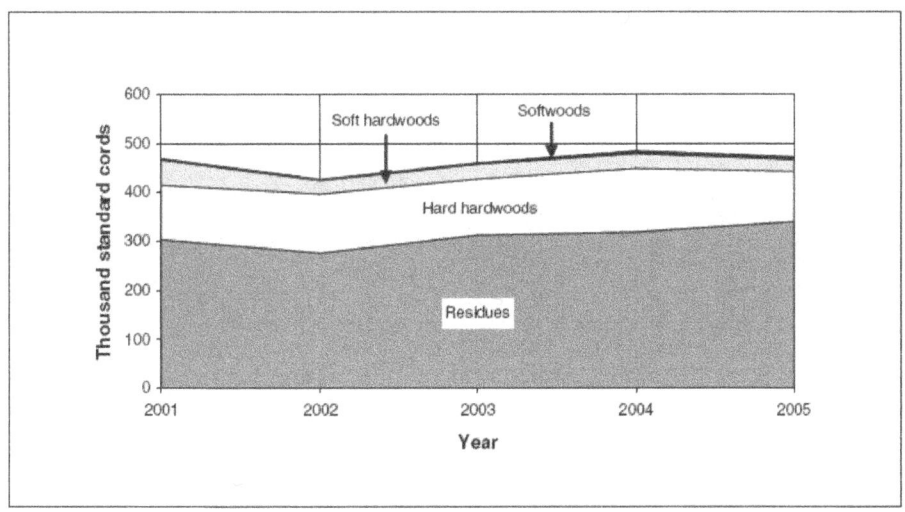

Figure 14.—Pulpwood production in the Central States, by species group and residues, 2001-05.

- Only 20 percent of the wood material produced for pulpwood in the Central States was processed by pulp and particleboard mills in the those states. Roundwood exports totaled 112 thousand cords, and the export of residues from primary wood-processing mills totaled 266 thousand cords.

- Loggers harvested pulpwood in 12 counties in Illinois, 21 counties in Indiana, and 9 counties in Missouri. There was no roundwood harvested for pulpwood from Iowa in 2005.

Illinois

- There are no primary wood-pulp or particleboard mills; consequently in Illinois, so all pulpwood harvested and residues produced by primary wood-processing mills, which are used by pulp or particleboard mills, are shipped to plants outside of the State. Illinois supplied 7 percent of the total wood material produced for pulpwood in the Central States.

- In 2005, Illinois produced 32 thousand cords of pulpwood, a decrease of more than 16 percent from the previous year (Fig. 15, Table 15).

Indiana

- In 2005, Indiana was the only state that had an increase in pulpwood production—20 higher than in 2004—and accounted for 40 percent of the total pulpwood produced in the Central States in 2005.

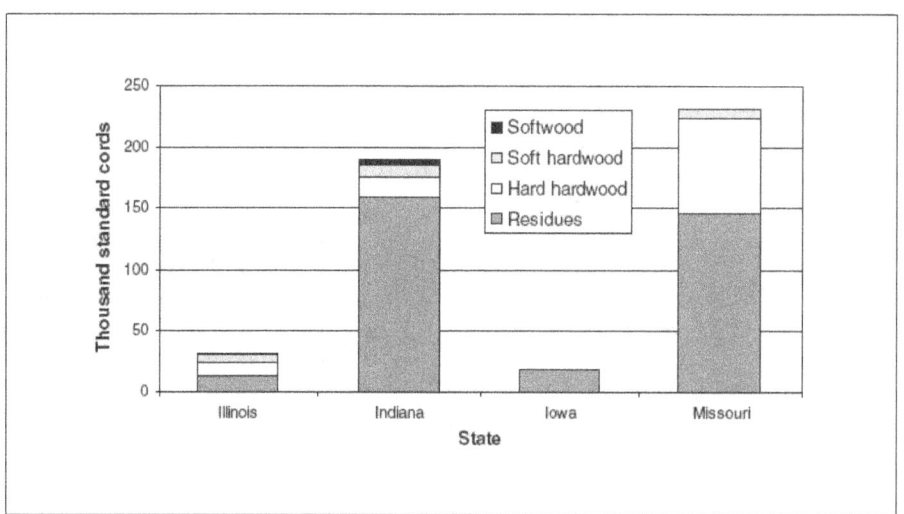

Figure 15.—Pulpwood production in the Central States, by state, species group, and residues, 2005.

- Roundwood production rose from 27 thousand cubic feet in 2004 to 31 thousand cubic feet in 2005, a 13-percent increase. Residues from Indiana primary wood processors that were used for pulpwood grew from 132 thousand cubic feet in 2004 to 159 thousand cubic feet in 2005, a 21-percent increase.

Iowa

- Total pulpwood production in Iowa in 2005 was 20 thousand cords, all coming from the residues of the State's primary wood processors. Iowa contributed 4 percent of the total pulpwood produced in the Central States.

- Iowa's total pulpwood production decreased by more than 20 percent between 2004 and 2005 because no roundwood was harvested for pulpwood in 2005.

Missouri

- Missouri remained the largest producer of pulpwood in the Central States in 2005 with nearly half of the regional total or 231 thousand cords. The production of pulpwood in Missouri decreased by 12 percent between 2004 and 2005.

- Missouri produced 85 thousand cords of roundwood and 146 thousand cords of residues for pulpwood in 2005. Ninety-four percent of this production is exported to mills in the Southern States.

RECEIPTS

Because of the limited number of pulp mills in the Central States, state-level receipts are not reported to avoid disclosure of individual mill receipts.

- Pulp mills in the Central States received 120 thousand cords in 2005, a decrease of 14 percent from 2004.

- Roundwood receipts decreased by nearly 30 percent, from 31 thousand cords in 2004 to 22 thousand cords in 2005. Residue receipts decreased by about 10 percent, from 108 thousand cords in 2004 to 97 thousand cords in 2005.

INDUSTRY TRENDS AND ANALYSIS

- Average daily wood-pulp production for pulp mills in the Central States fell from 564 tons per day in 2004 to 486 tons per day in 2005 (Table 16).

- In 2005, only 16 percent of the roundwood and 21 percent of the residues produced for pulpwood in the Central States went to pulp mills located in those States.

- Hardwood residues from sawmills and other wood-using mills accounted for 63 percent of all of the wood material used by the pulp mills in the Central States. These residues continue to be the largest component of the wood material procured.

PLAINS STATES

Because of the limited number of pulp mills in the Plains States, detailed production and receipts are not reported to avoid disclosure of individual mill receipts.

PRODUCTION

- In 2005, the Plains States produced 113 thousand cords of roundwood and mill residues for pulpwood production, only 3 thousand cords less than in 2004 (Fig. 16). Pulpwood came from North Dakota and South Dakota.

- Softwood residues accounted for more than half of the pulpwood production for the Plains States in 2005 (Fig. 17).

- In 2005, the only species harvested from the Plains States for pulpwood production were ponderosa pine, aspen, balsam poplar, and cottonwood.

- The only mill in the Plains States in 2004 was Merillat Corporation, LLC, Rapid City, SD, (particleboard), which has an annual production capacity of 95 million square feet (¾-inch basis).

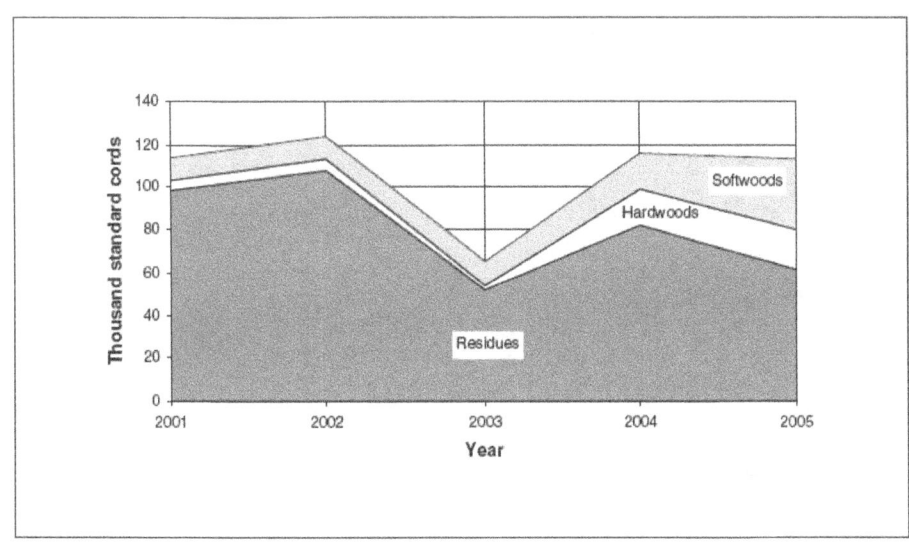

Figure 16.— Pulpwood production in the Plains States, by species group and residues, 2001-05.

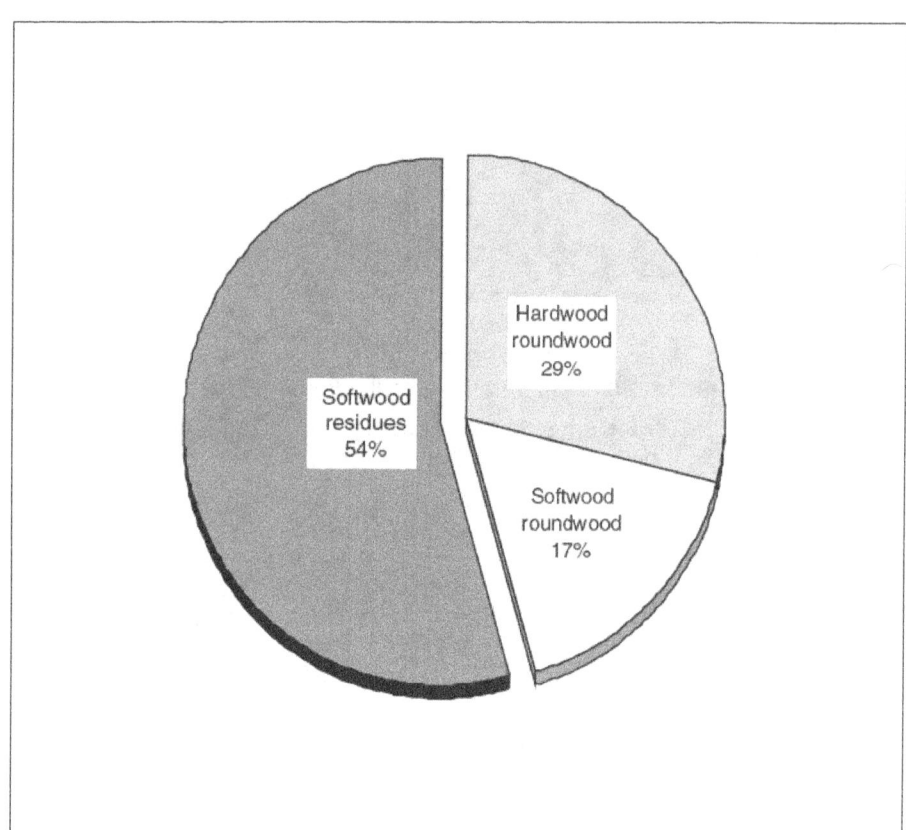

Figure 17.— Pulpwood production in the Plains States, by species group and residues, 2005.

APPENDIX

CONVERSION FACTORS USED
IN THE NORTH-CENTRAL REGION

(Standard cords of green roundwood per green ton)

Species	Factor	Species	Factor
Softwoods	0.4688	White birch	0.4018
Northern white-cedar	.6329	Yellow birch	.3723
Balsam fir	.4688	River birch	.3871
Hemlock	.4150	Sweetgum	.3669
Jack pine	.4688	Yellow-poplar	.4219
Red pine	.4688	Blackgum	.3779
White pine	.4777	Sycamore	.4083
Shortleaf pine	.3956	Cottonwood	.4291
Spruce	.5014	Elm	.4018
Tamarack	.4291	Hickory	.3701
Hardwoods	.3939	Hard maple	.3617
Soft hardwoods	.4171	Soft maple	.4083
Hard hardwoods	.3708	Black cherry	.4688
Ash	.4330	Red oak	.3444
Aspen	.4291	White oak	.3723
Balsam poplar	.4083	Black oak	.3444
Basswood	.5167	Other hardwoods	.4777
Beech	.3956		

LIST OF TABLES

TABLES

Table 3.--Production and imports of pulpwood, Lake States, 2005

(In standard cords, unpeeled)

Product form, species group, and destination	Production by state[1]			Regional total	Imports			Total imports	Total receipts
	Michigan	Minnesota	Wisconsin		Central States	Plains States	Canada		
Softwood roundwood									
Northern white-cedar									
Michigan	2,632	--	33	2,665	--	--	4	4	2,669
Total	2,632	--	33	2,665	--	--	4	4	2,669
Balsam fir									
Canada	4,973	1,290	--	6,263	--	--	--	--	--
Michigan	57,141	--	3,075	60,216	--	--	99	99	60,315
Minnesota	148	190,012	29,973	220,133	--	--	1,216	1,216	221,350
Wisconsin	2,310	184	67,597	70,091	--	--	41	41	70,132
Total	64,572	191,486	100,645	356,704	--	--	1,356	1,356	351,796
Hemlock									
Michigan	53,447	--	2,042	55,489	--	--	35	35	55,524
Wisconsin	3,359	--	33,281	36,641	--	--	--	--	36,641
Total	56,806	--	35,324	92,130	--	--	35	35	92,165
Jack pine									
Canada	197	488	--	685	--	--	--	--	--
Michigan	189,395	--	7,323	196,718	--	--	51	51	196,769
Minnesota	--	151,531	4,027	155,558	--	--	192	192	155,749
Wisconsin	11,650	2,499	175,484	189,632	16	--	80	96	189,728
Total	201,241	154,517	186,833	542,592	16	--	323	338	542,246
Red pine									
Canada	444	--	--	444	--	--	--	--	--
Michigan	53,388	--	10,031	63,419	--	--	578	578	63,998
Minnesota	--	40,226	3,861	44,087	--	--	--	--	44,087
Wisconsin	18,188	1,920	236,098	256,206	--	--	--	--	256,206
Total	72,019	42,146	249,991	364,156	--	--	578	578	364,290
White pine									
Canada	250	--	--	250	--	--	--	--	--
Michigan	5,580	--	1,546	7,125	--	--	9	9	7,134
Minnesota	--	2,072	224	2,296	--	--	--	--	2,296
Wisconsin	1,301	89	61,622	63,012	--	--	524	524	63,536
Total	7,131	2,160	63,392	72,683	--	--	533	533	72,966

Spruce								
Canada	7,460	1,499	--	8,959	--	--	--	--
Michigan	17,873	--	249	18,122	--	1,121	1,121	19,243
Minnesota	--	164,467	5,688	170,155	--	2,333	2,333	172,487
Wisconsin	38,613	18,288	56,700	113,601	--	10,117	10,117	123,718
Total	63,946	184,254	62,636	310,837	--	13,571	13,571	315,449
Tamarack								
Canada	--	1,169	--	1,169	--	--	--	--
Michigan	7,570	--	112	7,682	--	15	15	7,697
Minnesota	--	48,814	51	48,865	--	13	13	48,878
Wisconsin	4,588	12,194	15,751	32,533	--	2,429	2,429	34,962
Total	12,158	62,177	15,914	90,249	--	2,457	2,457	91,537
Other softwoods								
Michigan	4,774	--	--	4,774	--	--	--	4,774
Minnesota	--	955	--	955	--	--	--	955
Total	4,774	955	--	5,729	--	--	--	5,729
Total softwood roundwood								
Canada	13,324	4,446	--	17,770	--	--	--	--
Michigan	391,799	--	24,412	416,211	--	1,912	1,912	418,123
Minnesota	148	598,077	43,824	642,049	--	3,754	3,754	645,802
Wisconsin	80,009	35,174	646,533	761,715	16	13,191	13,207	774,922
Total	485,280	637,696	714,768	1,837,744	16	18,857	18,872	1,838,847
Softwood residues								
Canada	17,546	21,131	76	38,752	--	--	--	--
Michigan	158,338	--	662	159,001	--	--	--	159,001
Minnesota	--	88,337	1,623	89,960	--	--	--	89,960
Other States[2]	--	4,000	15,320	19,320	--	--	--	--
Wisconsin	29,082	1,607	137,949	168,638	34,248	14,442	48,690	217,328
Total	204,966	115,074	155,630	475,671	34,248	14,442	48,690	466,288
Total softwood material								
Canada	30,869	25,576	76	56,522	--	--	--	--
Michigan	550,138	--	25,074	575,212	--	1,912	1,912	577,124
Minnesota	148	686,413	45,447	732,008	--	3,754	3,754	735,762
Other States[2]	--	4,000	15,320	19,320	--	--	--	--
Wisconsin	109,091	36,781	784,482	930,353	34,264	27,633	61,897	992,250
Total	690,246	752,770	870,398	2,313,415	34,264	33,299	67,563	2,305,136

(Table 3 continued on next page)

(Table 3 continued)

Product form, species group, and destination	Production by state[1]				Imports			Total imports	Total receipts
	Michigan	Minnesota	Wisconsin	Regional total	Central States	Plains States	Canada		
Hardwood roundwood									
Ash									
Michigan	25,388	--	4,722	30,109	--	--	1,663	1,663	31,773
Minnesota	1,464	58,317	10,079	69,861	--	--	5,117	5,117	74,978
Wisconsin	8,997	51	76,335	85,382	--	--	1,137	1,137	86,520
Total	35,849	58,368	91,136	185,353	--	--	7,918	7,918	193,270
Aspen									
Canada	20	--	--	20	--	--	--	--	--
Michigan	794,169	--	91,033	885,202	--	--	52,709	52,709	937,911
Minnesota	6,001	1,775,517	99,774	1,881,293	--	25,959	217,679	243,638	2,124,931
Wisconsin	35,374	36,182	749,546	821,101	--	--	34,319	34,319	855,421
Total	835,564	1,811,699	940,353	3,587,616	--	25,959	304,708	330,667	3,918,262
Balsam poplar									
Michigan	32,734	--	216	32,950	--	--	407	407	33,357
Minnesota	156	110,773	2,144	113,072	--	478	15,597	16,075	129,147
Wisconsin	--	670	8	678	--	--	3,266	3,266	3,944
Total	32890	111442	2368	146700	--	478	19,270	19,748	166,448
Basswood									
Michigan	49,580	--	7,809	57,389	--	--	997	997	58,386
Minnesota	1,641	30,944	8,401	40,986	--	--	125	125	41,111
Wisconsin	4,568	882	65,884	71,333	--	--	--	--	71,333
Total	55,789	31,826	82,094	169,708	--	--	1,122	1,122	170,830
Beech									
Michigan	48,663	--	11,999	60,662	--	--	4,638	4,638	65,300
Wisconsin	360	--	2,216	2,576	--	--	3	3	2,578
Total	49,022	--	14,215	63,238	--	--	4,640	4,640	67,878
White birch									
Michigan	61,523	--	12,638	74,161	--	--	5,706	5,706	79,867
Minnesota	2,898	210,698	46,778	260,374	--	--	1,046	1,046	261,420
Wisconsin	29,074	47,419	222,479	298,971	--	--	8,644	8,644	307,615
Total	93,494	258,118	281,895	633,507	--	--	15,396	15,396	648,903
Yellow birch									
Michigan	24,691	--	7,842	32,533	--	--	2,876	2,876	35,409
Wisconsin	4,458	--	26,139	30,597	--	--	9	9	30,606
Total	29,149	--	33,981	63,131	--	--	2,884	2,884	66,015

Cottonwood									
Minnesota	--	333	34	367	--	--	6,097	6,097	6,464
Wisconsin	65	--	524	589	--	--	--	--	589
Total	65	333	558	955	--	--	6,097	6,097	7,053
Elm									
Michigan	1,622	--	--	1,622	--	--	0	0	1,622
Minnesota	1,072	1,163	3,271	5,505	--	--	16	16	5,522
Wisconsin	2,830	--	18,774	21,604	--	--	--	--	21,604
Total	5,524	1,163	22,044	28,731	--	--	16	16	28,747
Hickory									
Michigan	2,544	--	--	2,544	--	--	--	--	2,544
Wisconsin	131	--	1,050	1,181	--	--	--	--	1,181
Total	2,675	--	1,050	3,725	--	--	--	--	3,725
Hard maple									
Michigan	341,240	--	78,514	419,754	--	--	28,808	28,808	448,563
Minnesota	32,565	22,298	70,187	125,050	--	--	325	325	125,375
Wisconsin	34,225	5,903	330,800	370,929	--	--	6,811	6,811	377,740
Total	408,030	28,201	479,502	915,733	--	--	35,944	35,944	951,678
Soft maple									
Michigan	370,719	--	75,284	446,003	--	--	28,403	28,403	474,406
Minnesota	12,253	78,061	76,460	166,775	--	--	367	367	167,141
Wisconsin	34,639	782	279,061	314,482	--	--	5,659	5,659	320,142
Total	417,612	78,842	430,805	927,260	--	--	34,429	34,429	961,689
Red oak group									
Michigan	53,337	--	3,755	57,092	--	--	1,310	1,310	58,402
Minnesota	--	191	13	204	--	--	--	--	204
Wisconsin	2,879	267	166,213	169,359	--	--	5,626	5,626	174,985
Total	56,217	458	169,981	226,655	--	--	6,936	6,936	233,592
White oak group									
Michigan	22,095	--	--	22,095	--	--	--	--	22,095
Minnesota	--	232	14	245	--	--	--	--	245
Wisconsin	1,128	106	36,682	37,916	--	--	2,250	2,250	40,166
Total	23,223	338	36,695	60,257	--	--	2,250	2,250	62,507
Other hardwoods									
Michigan	18,502	--	4,847	23,350	--	--	1,831	1,831	25,181
Minnesota	1,275	1,382	3,888	6,545	--	--	19	19	6,565
Wisconsin	4	--	576	580	--	--	--	--	580
Total	19,781	1,382	9,312	30,475	--	--	1,850	1,850	32,325

(Table 3 continued on next page)

(Table 3 continued)

Product form, species group, and destination	Production by state[1]				Imports				Total receipts
	Michigan	Minnesota	Wisconsin	Regional total	Central States	Plains States	Canada	Total imports	
Total hardwood roundwood									
Canada	20	--	--	20	--	--	--	--	--
Michigan	1,846,806	--	298,660	2,145,466	--	--	129,348	129,348	2,274,814
Minnesota	59,325	2,289,910	321,044	2,670,278	--	32,534	240,291	272,825	2,943,103
Wisconsin	158,733	92,261	1,976,286	2,227,279	--	--	67,725	67,725	2,295,004
Total	2,064,884	2,382,171	2,595,989	7,043,044	--	32,534	437,364	469,898	7,512,922
Hardwood residues									
Canada	9,429	1,529	--	10,958	--	--	--	--	--
Michigan	148,206	--	10,215	158,421	3,531	--	30	3,562	161,983
Minnesota	--	23,572	2,632	26,204	--	--	18,633	18,633	44,837
Other States[2]	--	--	5,952	5,952	--	--	--	--	--
Wisconsin	6,276	6,316	245,064	257,656	2,002	--	--	2,002	259,658
Total	163,911	31,417	263,863	459,191	5,533	--	18,663	24,196	466,477
Total hardwood material									
Canada	9,449	1,529	--	10,978	--	--	--	--	--
Michigan	1,995,012	--	308,875	2,303,887	3,531	--	129,378	132,910	2,436,797
Minnesota	59,325	2,313,482	323,676	2,696,483	--	32,534	258,924	291,458	2,987,941
Other States[2]	--	--	5,952	5,952	--	--	--	--	--
Wisconsin	165,008	98,577	2,221,350	2,484,935	2,002	--	67,725	69,727	2,554,662
Total	2,228,795	2,413,588	2,859,853	7,502,235	5,533	32,534	456,028	494,094	7,979,399
Total all roundwood									
Canada	13,343	4,446	--	17,789	--	--	--	--	--
Michigan	2,238,606	--	323,072	2,561,677	--	--	131,260	131,260	2,692,937
Minnesota	59,473	2,887,986	364,867	3,312,327	--	32,534	244,045	276,579	3,588,906
Wisconsin	238,742	127,435	2,622,818	2,988,994	16	--	80,916	80,932	3,069,926
Total	2,550,164	3,019,867	3,310,757	8,880,788	16	32,534	456,221	488,771	9,351,769
Total all residues									
Canada	26,975	22,660	76	49,711	--	--	--	--	--
Michigan	306,544	--	10,877	317,422	3,531	--	30	3,562	320,983
Minnesota	--	111,909	4,255	116,164	--	--	18,633	18,633	134,797
Other States[2]	--	4,000	21,272	25,272	--	--	--	--	--
Wisconsin	35,358	7,923	383,013	426,294	36,250	--	14,442	50,692	476,986
Total	368,877	146,491	419,493	934,862	39,781	--	33,105	72,886	932,766

Total all wood material

Canada	40,318	27,106	76	67,500	--	--	--	--	--
Michigan	2,545,150	--	333,949	2,879,099	3,531	--	131,291	134,822	3,013,921
Minnesota	59,473	2,999,895	369,123	3,428,491	--	32,534	262,678	295,211	3,723,702
Other States²	--	4,000	21,272	25,272	--	--	--	--	--
Wisconsin	274,100	135,357	3,005,831	3,415,288	36,265	--	95,358	131,624	3,546,912
Total	2,919,041	3,166,358	3,730,251	9,815,650	39,797	32,534	489,327	561,657	10,284,535

¹ Includes amount of roundwood cut or residues generated by each state.

² Pulpwood shipped to mills outside of region.

All table cells without observations in the inventory sample are indicated by -- . Table value of 0 indicates the volume rounds to less than 1 standard cord, unpeeled. Columns and rows may not add to their totals due to rounding.

Table 4.—Lake States pulpwood production, by state of origin, year, and destination, 2001-05

(In thousand standard cords, unpeeled) [1]

Year	Total production	Destination of pulpwood			
		Michigan	Minnesota	Wisconsin	Other [2]
MICHIGAN					
2001	2,898	2,570	9	299	20
2002	2,900	2,615	10	254	21
2003	2,987	2,689	26	247	25
2004	3,105	2,691	60	311	43
2005	2,919	2,545	59	274	41
5-year average	2,962	2,622	33	277	30
MINNESOTA					
2001	2,839	--	2,630	187	22
2002	3,015	--	2,865	139	11
2003	2,958	--	2,757	191	10
2004	3,035	--	2,851	160	24
2005	3,166	--	3,000	135	31
5-year average	3,003	--	2,821	162	20
WISCONSIN					
2001	3,309	274	133	2,898	4
2002	3,485	256	360	2,864	6
2003	3,549	275	355	2,915	4
2004	3,684	268	332	3,080	4
2005	3,730	340	369	3,006	21
5-year average	3,551	283	310	2,953	8

[1] Includes mill residues used for pulp.

[2] Includes other states and Canada.

All table cells without observations in the inventory sample are indicated by -- .
Rows may not add to their totals due to rounding.

Table 5.—Lake States pulpwood production from roundwood, by state, Forest Inventory Unit and species group, 2001-05

(In thousand standard cords, unpeeled)

Forest Inventory Unit	All species					Pine					Spruce				
	2001	2002	2003	2004	2005	2001	2002	2003	2004	2005	2001	2002	2003	2004	2005
MICHIGAN															
Eastern Upper Peninsula	646	629	603	594	564	117	69	56	58	66	26	19	18	22	16
Western Upper Peninsula	959	933	953	1,035	965	59	46	40	46	76	32	27	27	46	42
Northern Lower Peninsula	789	829	874	951	972	106	74	100	150	137	2	1	4	6	6
Southern Lower Peninsula	53	61	68	78	49	1	2	2	4	2	--	--	--	0	0
Total	2,446	2,451	2,497	2,658	2,550	284	192	198	258	280	61	47	49	74	64
MINNESOTA															
Aspen-Birch	1,171	1,233	1,179	1,316	1,329	59	60	43	74	55	148	145	150	124	128
Northern Pine	1,318	1,373	1,350	1,295	1,439	63	88	75	118	133	51	69	67	40	55
Central Hardwoods	180	210	217	209	197	15	14	10	12	11	1	1	1	1	1
Prairie	86	91	84	56	55	0	0	1	1	0	0	0	0	0	0
Total	2,755	2,907	2,830	2,876	3,020	138	163	128	205	199	200	215	218	165	184
WISCONSIN															
Northeastern	1,001	994	1,079	1,167	1,200	115	88	109	84	147	24	19	26	26	28
Northwestern	1,159	1,340	1,311	1,309	1,354	168	134	103	90	96	15	25	30	26	28
Central	645	634	681	729	649	270	251	261	232	214	6	3	5	3	3
Southwestern	78	80	61	54	61	31	29	32	24	19	2	1	2	2	2
Southeastern	50	39	42	44	47	15	19	19	15	24	2	1	2	1	1
Total	2,932	3,087	3,174	3,302	3,311	600	521	524	445	500	49	49	65	58	63
Total Lake States	8,133	8,446	8,501	8,836	8,881	1,021	875	850	810	979	309	311	332	297	311

Forest Inventory Unit	Balsam fir					Other softwoods					Aspen				
	2001	2002	2003	2004	2005	2001	2002	2003	2004	2005	2001	2002	2003	2004	2005
MICHIGAN															
Eastern Upper Peninsula	26	33	26	35	27	40	32	33	33	23	153	160	149	134	139
Western Upper Peninsula	33	33	33	37	33	62	51	55	50	48	292	269	286	290	259
Northern Lower Peninsula	4	4	7	7	5	0	0	4	9	5	366	388	410	403	421
Southern Lower Peninsula	--	0	--	0	0	--	--	--	0	0	15	15	18	19	17
Total	64	70	66	79	65	103	84	91	92	76	826	832	863	846	836
MINNESOTA															
Aspen-Birch	101	94	93	117	128	25	20	37	22	33	699	754	632	723	703
Northern Pine	68	74	74	48	61	21	7	21	17	29	968	970	921	874	925
Central Hardwoods	1	1	1	2	3	0	0	0	1	1	147	156	168	146	134
Prairie	0	0	0	0	0	0	0	0	--	0	82	84	75	52	50
Total	171	169	168	167	191	46	28	59	40	63	1,895	1,965	1,796	1,794	1,812

(Table 5 continued on next page)

(Table 5 continued)

WISCONSIN

Balsam fir

Forest Inventory Unit	2001	2002	2003	2004	2005
Northeastern	35	31	25	32	48
Northwestern	48	39	45	44	51
Central	1	1	1	2	2
Southwestern	0	--	0	0	0
Southeastern	0	0	0	0	0
Total	84	71	71	78	101
Total Lake States	319	311	306	324	357

Other softwoods

Forest Inventory Unit	2001	2002	2003	2004	2005
Northeastern	24	22	31	29	32
Northwestern	7	13	10	12	13
Central	2	4	3	4	5
Southwestern	0	2	--	0	0
Southeastern	0	0	1	1	2
Total	33	40	46	46	51
Total Lake States	182	152	196	178	190

Aspen

Forest Inventory Unit	2001	2002	2003	2004	2005
Northeastern	291	290	320	343	320
Northwestern	415	546	479	440	444
Central	137	145	172	177	156
Southwestern	12	11	9	10	16
Southeastern	10	5	7	7	5
Total	865	996	987	976	940
Total Lake States	3,586	3,793	3,646	3,617	3,588

Birch

Forest Inventory Unit	2001	2002	2003	2004	2005
MICHIGAN					
Eastern Upper Peninsula	43	45	45	42	34
Western Upper Peninsula	68	71	73	76	68
Northern Lower Peninsula	31	28	25	29	20
Southern Lower Peninsula	0	1	1	1	1
Total	142	144	144	148	123
MINNESOTA					
Aspen-Birch	70	77	112	123	130
Northern Pine	71	77	91	94	106
Central Hardwoods	7	11	16	22	21
Prairie	0	1	1	1	1
Total	148	166	219	240	258
WISCONSIN					
Northeastern	91	95	100	123	108
Northwestern	110	119	128	162	170
Central	28	27	32	27	33
Southwestern	3	8	2	3	3
Southeastern	3	2	2	2	2
Total	235	251	264	316	316
Total Lake States	525	561	626	704	697

Maple

Forest Inventory Unit	2001	2002	2003	2004	2005
MICHIGAN					
Eastern Upper Peninsula	194	212	211	207	205
Western Upper Peninsula	308	340	339	374	353
Northern Lower Peninsula	196	239	222	234	251
Southern Lower Peninsula	16	19	22	23	16
Total	714	810	794	837	826
MINNESOTA					
Aspen-Birch	24	33	46	49	50
Northern Pine	18	25	34	32	42
Central Hardwoods	8	14	13	17	15
Prairie	--	0	0	0	0
Total	50	72	93	99	107
WISCONSIN					
Northeastern	287	332	340	381	372
Northwestern	258	333	361	376	388
Central	90	101	110	113	133
Southwestern	20	20	9	8	8
Southeastern	12	7	7	7	8
Total	666	793	826	884	910
Total Lake States	1,430	1,675	1,713	1,820	1,843

Other hardwoods

Forest Inventory Unit	2001	2002	2003	2004	2005
MICHIGAN					
Eastern Upper Peninsula	46	58	65	63	53
Western Upper Peninsula	104	95	100	116	87
Northern Lower Peninsula	83	95	102	112	127
Southern Lower Peninsula	20	23	25	32	13
Total	253	272	291	323	281
MINNESOTA					
Aspen-Birch	45	51	66	83	102
Northern Pine	58	62	69	72	90
Central Hardwoods	2	11	7	7	10
Prairie	4	6	7	3	4
Total	109	130	149	166	205
WISCONSIN					
Northeastern	132	118	129	149	146
Northwestern	138	131	155	161	164
Central	111	102	98	171	103
Southwestern	10	10	7	8	13
Southeastern	8	5	4	10	4
Total	400	366	392	499	429
Total Lake States	761	768	832	987	915

All table cells without observations in the inventory sample are indicated by --. Table value of 0 indicates the volume rounds to less than 1 thousand standard cords, unpeeled. Columns may not add to their totals due to rounding.

34

Table 6.—Lake States pulpwood production, by state of origin, product form, Forest Inventory Unit, and destination, 2005

(In thousand standard cords, unpeeled)

Product form and Forest Inventory Unit	Total production	Destination of pulpwood			
		Michigan	Minnesota	Wisconsin	Other[1]
MICHIGAN					
Roundwood					
Eastern Upper Peninsula	564	501	3	51	8
Western Upper Peninsula	965	724	56	185	0
Northern Lower Peninsula	972	964	--	2	5
Southern Lower Peninsula	49	49	--	--	--
Total	2550	2239	59	239	13
Residues	369	307	--	35	27
Total pulpwood	2919	2545	59	274	40
MINNESOTA					
Roundwood					
Aspen-Birch	1329	--	1247	77	4
Northern Pine	1439	--	1424	15	--
Central Hardwoods	197	--	162	35	--
Prairie	55	--	55	--	--
Total	3020	--	2888	127	4
Residues	146	--	112	8	27
Total pulpwood	3166	--	3000	135	31
WISCONSIN					
Roundwood					
Northeastern	1200	285	3	912	--
Northwestern	1354	34	360	960	--
Central	649	2	0	646	--
Southwestern	61	1	1	58	--
Southeastern	47	1	0	46	--
Total	3311	323	365	2623	--
Residues	419	11	4	383	21
Total pulpwood	3730	334	369	3006	21

[1] Includes other states and Canada.

All table cells without observations in the inventory sample are indicated by --. Table value of 0 indicates the volume rounds to less than 1 thousand standard cords, unpeeled. Columns and rows may not add to their totals due to rounding.

Table 7.—Pulpwood production from roundwood, by Forest Inventory Unit, county, and species group, Michigan, 2005

(In standard cords, unpeeled)

Forest Inventory Unit and county [1]	All species	Species group										
		Northern white-cedar	Balsam fir	Hemlock	Jack pine	Red pine	White pine	Spruce	Tamarack	Other softwoods	Ash	Aspen
Eastern Upper Peninsula												
Alger	63,042	173	3,953	4,245	3,182	2,525	333	1,717	581	--	764	8,112
Chippewa	83,363	57	2,545	2,438	5,328	3,001	183	2,297	192	--	681	35,342
Delta	98,824	225	5,266	3,075	2,515	3,777	434	2,665	756	--	1,141	19,032
Luce	69,634	92	3,448	1,843	16,447	1,240	200	3,180	307	--	961	14,508
Mackinac	70,471	68	1,581	655	7,277	2,928	461	482	212	--	691	22,645
Menominee	83,959	299	6,886	4,992	2,847	1,824	577	1,738	1,004	--	922	27,103
Schoolcraft	94,808	146	3,490	1,326	5,401	4,919	280	4,342	487	--	1,853	12,126
Total	564,101	1,061	27,170	18,574	42,997	20,214	2,468	16,421	3,538	--	7,013	138,868
Western Upper Peninsula												
Baraga	104,468	139	3,082	6,305	1,511	998	268	2,542	466	--	2,023	19,484
Dickinson	111,802	167	4,995	1,149	1,911	2,189	337	7,659	559	--	1,260	43,032
Gogebic	113,003	21	569	1,506	253	344	162	547	83	--	3,579	20,008
Houghton	103,267	44	2,791	7,513	2,693	5,816	972	2,836	227	--	2,774	25,954
Iron	124,912	252	7,730	2,406	3,125	5,981	588	15,876	857	--	1,966	41,702
Keweenaw	43,964	23	500	767	257	247	43	116	76	--	898	2,288
Marquette	240,687	509	11,485	13,973	23,678	21,197	992	10,395	6,188	--	1,676	62,985
Ontonagon	123,182	44	1,378	4,417	949	1,482	124	1,804	147	--	3,536	43,336
Total	965,285	1,199	32,531	38,036	34,377	38,252	3,487	41,775	8,603	--	17,712	258,788
Northern Lower Peninsula												
Alcona	36,197	20	157	--	1,198	86	7	38	--	169	209	26,171
Alpena	29,078	84	884	--	939	67	--	476	--	183	376	16,621
Antrim	34,793	--	--	--	5,111	237	58	--	--	667	455	9,484
Arenac	13,550	--	--	--	1,180	109	11	--	--	--	86	7,333
Bay	4,642	--	--	--	--	--	--	--	--	1	21	2,794
Benzie	16,717	--	15	--	681	667	2	2,324	--	356	518	4,080
Charlevoix	21,376	--	--	--	541	223	16	--	--	--	324	5,828
Cheboygan	62,703	101	1,019	--	6,791	380	86	508	--	323	542	32,602
Clare	48,663	--	--	--	3,551	525	18	--	--	--	492	23,641
Crawford	59,418	27	212	--	24,090	849	284	51	--	--	78	19,384
Emmet	25,309	6	53	--	617	93	11	13	--	210	332	9,611
Gladwin	32,775	--	--	--	3,928	215	32	--	--	--	200	14,262
Grand Traverse	13,581	--	--	--	2,011	446	10	--	--	743	179	4,096
Iosco	11,785	--	--	--	2,140	136	13	--	--	19	109	5,604
Isabella	12,088	--	--	--	107	265	--	--	--	--	79	7,270
Kalkaska	43,215	--	--	--	5,850	684	45	--	--	371	407	14,487
Lake	24,101	--	--	--	1,074	665	--	--	--	--	233	10,983
Leelanau	2,171	--	--	--	298	38	--	--	--	--	10	851

Manistee	23,951	--	--	--	684	618	3	--	--	22	713	8,367
Mason	19,982	--	--	--	533	624	--	--	--	--	540	8,596
Mecosta	22,889	--	--	88	870	465	--	--	--	--	345	12,038
Midland	20,693	--	--	--	644	64	--	--	--	--	101	11,139
Missaukee	36,021	--	--	--	2,511	254	14	--	--	--	408	16,858
Montmorency	63,103	12	658	--	11,502	271	112	864	--	18	476	33,051
Newaygo	22,966	--	--	--	322	106	--	--	--	--	358	7,421
Oceana	6,258	--	--	--	517	33	--	--	--	--	127	2,254
Ogemaw	42,525	--	--	--	12,378	255	111	--	--	138	460	15,504
Osceola	20,679	--	--	--	612	458	--	--	--	--	250	10,876
Oscoda	26,675	30	245	--	7,500	750	62	59	--	--	73	12,462
Otsego	57,761	1	198	3	3,756	575	71	283	2	1,387	970	17,290
Presque Isle	44,652	81	1,296	7	6,958	414	100	1,103	3	21	355	23,775
Roscommon	28,785	--	--	--	7,486	322	57	--	--	--	200	10,324
Wexford	42,723	--	--	--	5,975	2,246	44	--	--	147	749	15,845
Total	971,828	361	4,737	99	122,356	13,140	1,167	5,718	5	4,774	10,774	420,900
Southern Lower Peninsula												
Allegan	4,292	--	--	--	149	--	--	--	--	--	12	665
Barry	969	--	--	--	242	55	--	--	--	--	9	233
Calhoun	714	--	--	--	--	--	--	--	--	--	--	81
Clinton	429	4	82	97	177	30	7	19	12	--	--	--
Genesee	213	--	--	--	--	--	--	--	--	--	--	93
Gratiot	3,240	--	--	--	46	23	--	--	--	--	42	1,297
Huron	517	--	--	--	--	--	--	--	--	--	--	449
Ionia	1,198	--	--	--	--	--	--	--	--	--	4	596
Kalamazoo	2,626	--	--	--	--	--	--	--	--	--	--	296
Kent	7,351	--	--	--	--	--	--	--	--	--	99	1,979
Lapeer	177	--	--	--	148	--	--	--	--	--	--	29
Macomb	1,554	--	--	--	80	56	--	--	--	--	--	905
Montcalm	7,928	--	--	--	121	41	--	--	--	--	55	4,744
Muskegon	10,229	--	--	--	32	11	--	--	--	--	109	3,137
Ottawa	1,305	--	--	--	193	97	--	--	--	--	15	93
Saginaw	475	--	--	--	--	--	--	--	--	--	4	182
Sanilac	1,350	--	--	--	--	--	--	--	--	--	--	912
St. Joseph	401	--	--	--	--	100	--	--	--	--	--	45
Tuscola	2,075	--	--	--	246	--	--	--	--	--	--	1,079
Van Buren	1,689	--	--	--	--	--	--	--	--	--	--	191
Washtenaw	219	6	53	--	78	0	1	13	--	--	1	--
Total	48,951	10	135	97	1,512	413	8	32	12	--	350	17,007
State total	2,550,164	2,632	64,572	56,806	201,241	72,019	7,131	63,946	12,158	4,774	35,849	835,564

(Table 7 continued on next page)

(Table 7 continued)

Forest Inventory Unit and county [1]	Balsam poplar	Basswood	Beech	White birch	Yellow birch	Cottonwood	Elm	Hickory	Hard maple	Soft maple	Red oak group	White oak group	Other hardwoods
								Species group					
Eastern Upper Peninsula													
Alger	1,165	578	2,569	3,037	1,263	--	76	--	14,944	12,896	314	--	615
Chippewa	2,985	577	1,748	2,624	988	--	75	--	10,803	10,635	331	--	532
Delta	1,568	967	4,151	4,128	2,135	--	19	--	23,710	21,387	703	--	1,168
Luce	1,827	507	985	3,381	561	--	245	--	10,231	7,897	1,131	448	192
Mackinac	2,091	489	2,022	2,522	1,116	--	29	--	12,167	11,999	407	--	628
Menominee	1,109	1,646	2,176	3,508	1,185	--	159	--	13,159	11,929	363	8	525
Schoolcraft	966	1,011	3,172	5,715	1,898	--	249	--	22,680	20,910	2,240	672	926
Total	11,711	5,775	16,824	24,916	9,147	--	852	--	107,695	97,654	5,489	1,128	4,586
Western Upper Peninsula													
Baraga	2,033	1,752	3,853	7,074	2,231	--	418	--	27,212	21,626	556	--	898
Dickinson	840	5,012	2,366	5,925	1,546	--	189	--	16,024	15,300	547	--	795
Gogebic	90	4,762	1,682	8,478	2,717	44	1,249	89	40,348	24,030	1,047	--	1,395
Houghton	461	2,048	1,975	5,155	2,592	--	169	--	22,874	14,761	1,064	--	550
Iron	396	2,739	1,669	7,917	1,525	1	491	2	14,516	14,339	323	--	510
Keweenaw	10	550	2,410	2,467	1,528	--	--	--	15,190	14,915	713	--	966
Marquette	3,623	1,594	6,197	6,995	2,812	--	179	--	35,869	28,628	478	--	1,233
Ontonagon	503	4,112	1,384	5,609	3,196	20	442	41	33,858	13,971	2,166	--	663
Total	7,954	22,569	21,535	49,620	18,147	65	3,137	131	205,892	147,571	6,892	--	7,011
Northern Lower Peninsula													
Alcona	1,206	316	201	737	1	--	0	--	663	3,855	967	32	166
Alpena	661	546	361	1,198	1	--	1	--	1,191	4,047	1,233	27	180
Antrim	484	2,221	425	1,717	92	--	89	138	5,533	6,578	264	509	732
Arenac	268	79	84	78	1	--	0	--	377	3,287	600	31	25
Bay	1	23	35	72	1	--	1	--	273	1,394	1	1	23
Benzie	69	251	468	26	12	--	14	24	3,772	2,562	107	99	670
Charlevoix	539	2,492	312	626	100	--	119	179	3,431	5,595	341	659	50
Cheboygan	746	3,307	727	1,947	196	--	12	5	5,017	7,928	92	18	357
Clare	409	447	532	157	72	--	79	140	4,624	9,675	2,981	999	323
Crawford	90	306	106	1,105	35	--	30	30	1,286	10,334	989	132	0
Emmet	120	2,818	427	1,230	80	--	13	0	4,304	5,038	52	6	276
Gladwin	166	235	182	115	29	--	32	56	1,604	7,868	2,988	755	108
Grand Traverse	165	184	167	64	29	--	32	57	1,500	1,802	910	363	824
Iosco	102	19	106	280	1	--	--	1	406	2,792	14	6	36
Isabella	232	139	53	90	41	--	45	80	640	2,493	199	345	8
Kalkaska	1,003	1,999	312	745	184	--	192	338	5,947	8,417	642	1,241	352
Lake	236	301	191	74	68	--	--	66	1,830	3,500	3,667	1,128	85
Leelanau	20	29	6	7	6	--	--	6	450	356	47	48	--

Manistee	10	250	655	4	2	--	2	4	4,845	2,743	3,818	735	477
Mason	179	257	478	69	31	--	35	62	3,729	2,798	1,287	449	316
Mecosta	391	335	282	150	69	--	75	133	2,484	3,393	934	685	153
Midland	276	211	87	582	57	--	59	95	909	5,940	181	348	--
Missaukee	565	503	326	227	100	--	109	193	3,436	8,666	883	810	158
Montmorency	994	2,329	482	1,625	9	--	6	--	4,058	6,222	383	7	23
Newaygo	407	301	323	157	72	--	79	140	2,829	3,446	5,159	1,672	172
Oceana	181	117	101	70	32	--	35	62	932	1,289	173	288	48
Ogemaw	338	235	427	322	7	--	7	12	2,617	6,393	2,463	509	347
Osceola	310	299	207	118	54	--	60	105	2,697	3,331	711	483	107
Oscoda	107	1,241	73	111	0	--	0	--	1,830	1,978	134	18	3
Otsego	523	3,553	1,149	2,703	181	--	97	94	10,239	12,151	671	356	1,509
Presque Isle	899	721	381	1,773	17	--	11	--	1,685	4,820	207	2	21
Roscommon	284	183	85	212	52	--	57	98	971	3,995	3,457	984	18
Wexford	252	559	675	165	45	--	49	85	5,371	4,771	2,204	2,963	578
Total	12,236	26,804	10,427	18,556	1,680	--	1,342	2,203	91,482	159,457	38,757	16,708	8,145
Southern Lower Peninsula													
Allegan	40	21	7	16	7	--	8	14	96	1,328	917	1,013	--
Barry	31	16	6	12	6	--	6	11	73	211	20	39	--
Calhoun	--	--	--	--	--	--	--	--	--	230	194	210	--
Clinton	--	--	--	--	--	--	--	--	--	--	--	--	--
Genesee	--	--	--	--	--	--	--	--	2	118	--	--	--
Gratiot	145	74	26	56	25	--	28	50	359	790	95	184	--
Huron	--	--	--	--	--	--	--	--	53	16	--	--	--
Ionia	14	7	3	5	3	--	3	5	33	498	9	18	18
Kalamazoo	--	--	--	--	--	--	--	--	--	846	713	771	--
Kent	242	132	70	63	43	--	47	83	772	2,287	669	817	18
Lapeer	--	--	--	--	--	--	--	--	--	--	--	--	--
Macomb	--	--	--	--	--	--	--	--	11	502	--	--	--
Montcalm	175	181	36	71	31	--	34	60	450	1,324	247	356	3
Muskegon	329	170	72	127	58	--	64	113	966	2,510	1,413	1,108	8
Ottawa	--	5	14	--	--	--	--	--	101	314	224	242	10
Saginaw	14	7	2	5	2	--	3	5	33	192	9	17	--
Sanilac	--	--	--	--	--	--	--	--	--	438	--	--	--
St. Joseph	--	--	--	--	--	--	--	--	--	129	109	118	--
Tuscola	--	25	--	--	--	--	--	--	5	619	--	--	--
Van Buren	--	--	--	--	--	--	--	--	--	544	459	496	--
Washtenaw	--	3	1	17	0	--	0	--	9	37	--	--	--
Total	989	640	237	402	176	--	193	341	2,962	12,931	5,078	5,388	39
State total	32,890	55,789	49,022	93,494	29,149	65	5,524	2,675	408,030	417,612	56,217	23,223	19,781

[1] Includes only those counties that supplied pulpwood in 2005.

All table cells without observations in the inventory sample are indicated by --. Table value of 0 indicates the volume rounds to less than 1 standard cord, unpeeled. Columns and rows may not add to their totals due to rounding.

Table 8.—Pulpwood production from roundwood, by Forest Inventory Unit, county, and species group, Minnesota, 2005

(In standard cords, unpeeled)

Forest Inventory Unit and county [1]	All species	Balsam fir	Jack pine	Red pine	White pine	Spruce	Tamarack	Other softwoods	Ash	Aspen
Aspen-Birch										
Carlton	75,589	5,645	1,822	1,739	83	1,856	463	--	1,252	39,224
Cook	30,904	1,318	196	472	4	4,994	939	--	65	20,799
Koochiching	365,294	29,903	8,723	962	166	45,853	18,239	--	13,955	189,729
Lake	92,355	8,156	2,382	2,856	53	7,755	236	--	1,238	39,241
St. Louis	764,793	83,169	25,851	8,676	611	67,512	13,223	--	16,017	414,489
Total	1,328,935	128,190	38,975	14,704	917	127,971	33,100	--	32,527	703,482
Northern Pine										
Aitkin	173,455	7,745	4,006	2,651	233	8,244	2,565	--	2,363	114,454
Becker	51,210	1,360	3,181	451	1	128	243	41	108	40,500
Beltrami	206,925	6,569	16,677	1,211	11	3,764	5,014	--	4,119	140,194
Cass	149,884	4,038	8,037	3,200	117	1,592	932	--	1,417	101,922
Clearwater	77,442	2,024	3,505	178	1	1,020	1,355	--	540	61,165
Crow Wing	104,643	755	6,681	2,638	138	295	227	--	1,701	70,981
Hubbard	143,581	408	40,829	2,787	14	573	376	80	414	87,640
Itasca	342,996	33,499	6,407	5,810	112	31,446	5,125	412	7,069	196,205
Lake of the Woods	88,876	3,132	5,756	370	1	5,767	10,471	--	3,512	46,067
Mahnomen	17,076	86	1,569	25	--	117	199	--	161	13,176
Roseau	55,462	882	2,392	844	--	1,927	1,285	--	1,386	38,531
Wadena	27,239	28	11,064	1,617	--	--	255	--	15	13,713
Total	1,438,789	60,524	110,105	21,782	629	54,873	28,046	534	22,804	924,550
Central Hardwood										
Anoka	45	--	--	--	--	13	--	--	--	11
Benton	2,123	--	34	29	--	--	19	--	3	1,982
Chisago	822	9	24	23	--	--	0	--	3	568
Dakota	68	--	--	--	--	56	--	--	--	12
Douglas	563	211	17	20	--	38	--	--	--	272
Fillmore	12	12	--	--	--	--	--	--	--	--
Goodhue	108	10	--	--	--	--	--	--	5	--
Houston	4,652	84	148	--	--	151	195	--	254	2,721
Isanti	2,353	10	44	539	12	--	--	48	--	1,269

County										
Kanabec	21,420	9	517	279	23	--	62	--	367	16,010
Mille Lacs	18,989	158	285	188	77	151	26	22	266	13,682
Morrison	28,169	94	685	293	126	35	22	37	162	23,462
Olmsted	70	--	7	50	--	3	--	--	--	9
Otter Tail	11,267	--	941	21	--	496	220	48	53	9,367
Pine	96,925	1,505	2,378	2,482	147	--	--	--	1,402	58,866
Ramsey	12	--	--	--	--	--	--	--	--	12
Sherburne	1,288	5	73	268	228	--	1	266	6	371
Stearns	60	--	3	1	--	--	0	--	2	35
Todd	3,989	--	--	12	--	--	--	--	--	3,658
Wabasha	1,143	--	21	1,122	--	--	--	--	--	--
Washington	2,265	482	6	3	0	150	0	--	4	1,580
Winona	528	--	--	324	--	--	147	--	--	12
Wright	211	--	11	5	0	--	1	--	7	121
Total	197,081	2,591	5,193	5,659	615	1,093	694	421	2,537	134,019
Prairie										
Kittson	13,678	112	196	--	--	202	260	--	324	11,388
Marshall	24,967	28	49	--	--	109	77	--	102	22,508
Norman	1,662	--	--	--	--	--	--	--	--	1,651
Pennington	3,451	10	--	--	--	7	--	--	--	3,379
Polk	9,674	5	--	--	--	--	--	--	73	9,191
Red Lake	1,629	27	--	--	--	--	--	--	--	1,532
Total	55,061	182	245	--	--	318	337	--	499	49,648
State total	3,019,867	191,486	154,517	42,146	2,160	184,254	62,177	955	58,368	1,811,699

(Table 8 continued on next page)

(Table 8 continued)

Forest Inventory Unit and county[1]	Species group									
	Balsam poplar	Basswood	White birch	Cotton-wood[2]	Elm	Hard maple	Soft maple	Red oak group	White oak group	Other hardwoods
Aspen-Birch										
Carlton	650	2,134	13,702	--	110	2,362	4,418	--	--	131
Cook	37	61	1,753	--	6	59	195	--	--	7
Koochiching	32,004	1,002	24,424	--	4	39	285	--	--	5
Lake	1,830	1,718	19,124	--	71	1,625	5,986	--	--	84
St. Louis	24,013	4,317	71,066	20	327	11,880	23,102	93	36	389
Total	58,533	9,231	130,069	20	518	15,965	33,986	93	36	616
Northern Pine										
Aitkin	2,361	3,312	12,216	--	185	2,252	10,507	67	72	220
Becker	340	527	4,085	--	1	10	233	--	--	1
Beltrami	12,909	3,482	11,173	--	15	152	1,619	--	--	18
Cass	2,810	1,613	17,102	--	41	413	6,602	--	--	49
Clearwater	1,144	1,786	4,389	30	1	13	292	--	--	1
Crow Wing	765	2,235	9,735	--	149	1,530	6,620	8	8	178
Hubbard	724	1,232	7,498	--	3	33	965	--	--	4
Itasca	12,521	2,797	31,164	--	59	1,930	8,369	--	--	71
Lake of the Woods	7,713	24	5,961	--	2	22	74	--	--	3
Mahnomen	689	670	382	--	--	--	1	--	--	--
Roseau	5,942	--	2,272	1	--	--	--	--	--	--
Wadena	149	17	382	--	--	--	--	--	--	--
Total	48,068	17,694	106,358	31	458	6,355	35,280	74	80	544
Central Hardwood										
Anoka	--	--	22	--	--	--	--	--	--	--
Benton	2	3	37	--	0	3	10	--	--	0
Chisago	1	4	117	--	0	38	33	--	--	0
Dakota	--	--	--	--	--	--	--	--	--	--
Douglas	4	--	--	--	--	--	--	--	--	--
Fillmore	--	--	--	--	--	--	--	--	--	--
Goodhue	--	--	5	--	--	29	24	24	10	--
Houston	477	--	416	--	--	70	57	57	23	--
Isanti	--	196	43	--	--	50	104	18	19	--

County										
Kanabec	666	159	1,832	--	31	321	1,105	--	--	37
Mille Lacs	950	92	956	--	17	370	1,630	46	50	21
Morrison	491	115	1,647	--	14	207	685	24	51	17
Olmsted	--	--	--	--	--	--	--	--	--	--
Otter Tail	622	149	61	--	--	--	6	--	--	--
Pine	1,744	1,024	15,584	--	122	4,764	5,856	122	68	145
Ramsey	--	--	--	--	--	--	--	--	--	--
Sherburne	6	5	28	--	0	6	24	--	--	0
Stearns	2	1	8	--	--	2	7	--	--	--
Todd	172	10	136	--	--	--	--	--	--	--
Wabasha	--	--	--	--	--	--	--	--	--	--
Washington	4	2	16	--	0	4	13	--	--	0
Winona	--	--	33	--	--	11	--	--	--	--
Wright	7	3	27	--	0	7	22	--	--	0
Total	4,866	2,046	20,969	--	187	5,881	9,576	291	221	222
Prairie										
Kittson	5	648	544	--	--	--	--	--	--	--
Marshall	18	1,928	148	--	--	--	--	--	--	--
Norman	--	11	--	--	--	--	--	--	--	--
Pennington	--	55	--	--	--	--	--	--	--	--
Polk	--	95	29	281	--	--	--	--	--	--
Red Lake	12	58	--	--	--	--	--	--	--	--
Total	35	2,795	722	281	--	--	--	--	--	--
State total	31,826	111,442	258,118	333	1,163	28,201	78,842	458	338	1,382

[1] Includes only those counties that supplied pulpwood in 2005.

[2] Includes hybrid poplar.

All table cells without observations in the inventory sample are indicated by -- . Table value of 0 indicates the volume rounds to less than 1 standard cord, unpeeled. Columns and rows may not add to their totals due to rounding.

Table 9.—Pulpwood production from roundwood, by Forest Inventory Unit, county, and species group, Wisconsin, 2005

(In standard cords, unpeeled)

Forest Inventory Unit and county[1]	All species	Species group										
		Northern white-cedar	Balsam fir	Hemlock	Jack pine	Red pine	White pine	Spruce	Tamarack	Ash	Aspen	Balsam poplar
Northeastern												
Florence	89,442	17	2,924	3,944	4,523	4,441	497	1,099	196	1,808	16,740	56
Forest	144,847	7	5,764	756	486	2,309	151	3,315	285	5,295	31,407	22
Langlade	186,502	--	8,046	434	346	2,404	261	4,680	1,066	7,054	38,547	1
Lincoln	152,093	--	4,665	779	905	2,327	624	2,633	278	5,563	50,847	--
Marinette	150,356	9	4,985	2,191	12,543	10,975	1,744	2,689	347	3,091	52,220	94
Menominee	51,981	--	238	12,843	681	2,596	2,160	46	1	1,521	8,355	--
Oconto	85,335	--	1,045	719	14,029	15,213	1,663	1,482	15	1,173	28,096	--
Oneida	195,395	--	16,335	872	14,965	18,677	4,397	9,932	3,179	3,634	60,724	--
Shawano	64,357	--	1,287	3,044	1,064	12,586	1,290	99	182	2,665	6,120	23
Vilas	79,981	--	2,247	107	6,634	4,333	2,164	1,872	311	1,916	27,070	0
Total	1,200,289	33	47,535	25,688	56,176	75,861	14,952	27,846	5,861	33,720	320,128	196
Northwestern												
Ashland	219,871	--	7,092	143	6,557	3,155	388	4,241	1,703	6,507	70,297	787
Barron	27,554	--	190	22	1,085	1,013	515	33	81	581	13,122	6
Bayfield	147,106	--	6,107	8	4,990	7,545	493	3,119	26	3,711	46,077	393
Burnett	55,381	--	137	--	8,685	2,826	962	--	431	885	23,553	79
Douglas	135,658	--	11,153	--	17,672	7,459	616	1,652	304	2,558	37,345	340
Iron	81,894	--	2,882	74	434	373	985	1,617	375	3,484	16,899	122
Polk	14,599	--	120	--	611	397	91	61	--	352	6,912	3
Price	146,572	--	11,819	3,564	405	1,340	366	7,617	4,096	4,594	41,941	27
Rusk	76,264	--	819	26	102	1,304	263	3,157	269	2,583	28,059	29
Sawyer	249,101	--	6,548	27	1,469	3,334	1,527	4,466	558	8,646	78,714	251
Taylor	87,628	--	2,144	895	--	628	73	1,824	278	3,495	31,950	--
Washburn	112,587	--	2,378	--	11,032	5,880	1,045	353	295	2,676	49,122	101
Total	1,354,214	--	51,390	4,759	53,042	35,254	7,323	28,141	8,416	40,071	443,991	2,137
Central												
Adams	63,990	--	--	--	18,611	20,863	5,649	55	147	597	3,880	--
Chippewa	37,068	--	25	7	264	1,798	300	737	214	1,049	17,787	0
Clark	62,100	--	--	--	3,115	1,985	925	148	--	1,412	32,066	1
Eau Claire	23,207	--	--	--	2,916	3,067	690	15	--	630	4,685	--
Jackson	60,514	--	9	--	10,983	8,178	3,041	48	16	1,431	8,920	--
Juneau	55,657	--	--	--	16,001	12,839	3,146	--	--	902	5,441	--
Marathon	104,797	--	1,117	3,367	573	6,787	1,041	864	16	4,912	30,382	--
Marquette	11,129	--	3	--	711	6,204	917	204	31	88	235	--
Monroe	27,758	--	--	--	5,900	3,016	1,714	58	101	420	3,126	--
Portage	46,183	--	315	393	8,148	8,506	3,767	81	42	1,083	8,243	--
Waupaca	35,037	--	46	79	175	11,857	2,704	373	92	957	6,593	--
Waushara	45,035	--	--	--	1,492	14,454	2,724	323	--	461	2,135	--
Wood	76,334	--	30	25	5,932	8,713	4,771	365	16	1,487	32,430	1
Total	648,808	--	1,545	3,870	74,822	108,268	31,388	3,272	675	15,428	155,923	2

Southwestern													
Buffalo	3,042	—	—	113	—	—	293	110	—	—	72	859	—
Crawford	1,392	—	—	—	—	—	221	245	—	—	42	108	—
Dunn	17,467	—	7	1,178	—	—	3,243	517	327	—	290	4,956	0
Grant	1,335	—	—	—	—	—	841	140	152	—	7	105	—
Iowa	3,187	—	—	49	—	—	996	718	104	—	46	408	—
La Crosse	4,006	—	—	136	—	—	1,052	177	226	—	44	1,574	—
Lafayette	28	—	—	—	—	—	—	—	—	—	2	—	—
Pepin	663	—	—	—	—	—	30	33	27	—	1	422	—
Pierce	2,658	—	—	26	—	—	47	35	—	—	15	685	—
Richland	2,617	—	—	21	—	—	217	532	—	—	108	324	—
Sauk	7,029	—	40	609	—	—	2,669	484	630	—	88	761	—
St. Croix	5,471	—	—	29	—	—	319	24	189	—	61	3,578	2
Trempealeau	8,798	—	—	230	—	—	2,514	767	293	—	97	1,308	—
Vernon	2,952	—	—	31	—	—	406	192	—	—	15	438	—
Total	60,643	—	47	2,422	—	—	12,847	3,975	1,958	—	888	15,526	2
Southeastern													
Brown	2,190	—	11	78	—	—	1,513	64	—	—	26	159	—
Calumet	172	—	53	—	—	—	—	—	—	—	9	28	—
Columbia	4,871	—	—	77	—	—	2,157	293	23	—	113	311	—
Dane	511	—	—	16	—	—	83	100	47	—	6	39	—
Dodge	474	—	—	—	—	—	—	69	22	—	25	40	—
Door	9,916	—	49	—	989	—	413	2,140	315	—	296	2,519	10
Fond Du Lac	251	—	—	—	—	—	—	—	61	—	8	—	—
Green	1,107	—	—	164	—	—	355	329	83	—	37	14	—
Green Lake	335	—	—	—	—	—	40	—	—	—	5	15	—
Jefferson	247	—	—	—	—	—	—	35	196	—	3	—	—
Kenosha	319	—	—	—	—	—	137	—	59	—	—	—	—
Kewaunee	6,962	—	—	—	—	—	5,025	285	34	—	101	479	8
Manitowoc	2,465	—	15	—	—	—	119	450	—	962	57	39	—
Outagamie	10,938	—	—	—	—	—	6,279	265	—	—	218	893	11
Ozaukee	1,874	—	—	—	—	—	889	853	—	—	13	—	—
Rock	100	—	—	—	—	—	—	—	—	—	5	—	—
Sheboygan	1,207	—	—	—	—	—	425	92	452	—	17	25	—
Walworth	91	—	—	—	—	—	—	—	28	—	—	63	—
Washington	787	—	—	16	—	—	125	16	66	—	40	28	—
Waukesha	395	—	—	—	—	—	151	36	2	—	15	—	—
Winnebago	1,591	—	—	—	18	—	186	590	31	—	34	135	—
Total	46,803	—	129	371	1,006	—	17,760	5,754	1,419	962	1,029	4,785	30
State total	3,310,757	33	100,645	186,833	35,324	1,006	249,991	63,392	62,636	15,914	91,136	940,353	2,368

(Table 9 continued on next page)

(Table 9 continued)

Forest Inventory Unit and county [1]	Species group											
	Basswood	Beech	White birch	Yellow birch	Cotton-wood	Elm	Hickory	Hard maple	Soft maple	Red oak group	White oak group	Other hardwoods
Northeastern												
Florence	1,660	2,729	5,255	2,011	--	260	--	19,473	19,384	1,283	53	1,090
Forest	7,546	2,628	14,996	3,313	10	1,321	20	30,257	30,254	3,287	313	1,105
Langlade	10,937	2,867	18,385	3,670	20	1,693	40	39,222	36,700	7,756	1,249	1,125
Lincoln	5,388	458	11,157	3,822	202	1,719	403	33,643	21,760	4,219	611	88
Marinette	6,544	1,508	8,926	1,946	--	756	--	19,016	17,527	2,383	245	618
Menominee	2,520	196	2,707	714	25	359	50	8,240	5,710	2,692	289	38
Oconto	720	823	2,556	841	--	165	--	8,352	7,349	732	64	298
Oneida	3,075	881	11,205	2,581	72	1,354	145	18,177	17,277	6,838	734	339
Shawano	1,047	203	3,257	656	5	245	11	13,902	9,532	5,564	1,566	9
Vilas	1,225	119	9,205	964	30	622	59	9,535	7,010	4,066	472	21
Total	40,662	12,411	87,649	20,518	365	8,494	728	199,818	172,502	38,820	5,595	4,731
Northwestern												
Ashland	4,652	73	25,932	967	2	2,093	4	39,572	37,862	5,235	1,148	1,463
Barron	1,001	1	1,663	104	1	96	2	2,170	3,034	2,197	624	11
Bayfield	2,645	16	20,495	757	16	1,202	31	21,498	21,446	4,768	1,049	717
Burnett	695	--	5,215	50	--	171	--	4,137	5,276	1,715	421	144
Douglas	2,130	3	19,091	266	3	760	6	16,150	16,153	1,081	295	621
Iron	2,233	212	13,021	1,408	18	1,155	38	17,200	16,043	2,429	514	380
Po k	262	--	1,530	102	--	106	--	1,353	1,809	708	175	6
Price	3,731	466	17,165	2,374	45	1,679	91	20,116	18,687	5,509	724	216
Rusk	2,329	10	8,103	495	5	479	9	9,963	10,286	6,104	1,818	51
Sawyer	7,199	266	27,547	1,906	5	1,962	11	40,117	38,730	19,380	5,838	598
Taylor	3,039	111	10,632	1,225	24	957	47	15,370	11,856	2,548	509	23
Washburn	4,618	--	9,300	276	34	407	--	8,358	10,809	4,443	1,296	164
Total	34,535	1,159	159,695	9,930	153	11,066	240	196,004	191,990	56,118	14,410	4,391
Central												
Adams	49	1	798	32	--	31	--	3,280	2,816	5,803	1,375	2
Chippewa	769	9	3,779	276	1	264	1	3,091	3,571	2,664	450	10
Clark	949	22	3,972	325	3	294	5	5,957	5,349	4,450	1,117	5
Eau Claire	277	3	1,753	175	1	171	1	2,202	2,292	3,716	614	1
Jackson	328	2	2,869	191	2	173	3	7,159	6,445	8,361	2,356	--
Juneau	104	--	1,028	19	--	19	--	5,242	4,422	4,738	1,756	1
Marathon	2,150	380	4,470	846	10	525	22	25,044	15,284	5,604	1,304	99
Marquette	7	1	132	23	1	11	2	507	420	1,387	244	--
Monroe	44	--	4,721	22	--	21	--	3,391	2,009	2,418	798	--
Portage	405	25	2,062	180	--	182	--	4,770	4,111	2,937	918	14
Waupaca	475	60	1,436	226	2	147	5	4,619	3,120	1,833	239	--
Waushara	13	12	614	160	9	61	19	2,950	2,314	15,180	2,114	--
Wood	563	23	2,658	276	--	193	--	6,785	6,109	4,512	1,393	51
Total	6,134	539	30,292	2,750	29	2,093	58	74,997	58,263	63,602	14,676	183

46

Southwestern

County											
Buffalo	21	--	260	17	--	15	1	326	355	494	107	--
Crawford	5	--	61	3	--	3	--	233	203	183	73	--
Dunn	348	1	911	102	1	94	2	1,140	1,533	2,477	338	1
Grant	4	--	23	2	--	2	--	23	25	9	2	--
Iowa	3	--	56	2	--	2	--	270	228	218	86	--
La Crosse	14	--	102	16	--	11	1	207	185	213	48	--
Lafayette	1	--	4	--	--	--	--	12	7	1	--	--
Pepin	1	--	3	--	--	--	--	3	7	122	14	--
Pierce	5	1	43	18	1	7	2	98	75	1,441	159	--
Richland	53	--	322	32	--	32	--	360	392	171	52	--
Sauk	11	1	134	9	--	7	--	459	399	584	143	--
St. Croix	35	2	168	19	--	18	--	211	699	96	17	5
Trempealeau	42	1	375	44	1	30	2	407	386	2,041	260	--
Vernon	1	1	28	16	1	5	2	109	78	1,459	170	--
Total	543	7	2,492	279	4	227	10	3,859	4,573	9,509	1,469	6

Southeastern

County											
Brown	14	0	76	10	--	8	--	87	85	50	6	--
Calumet	--	1	--	--	--	--	--	56	25	--	--	--
Columbia	23	3	248	64	3	32	6	625	516	281	96	--
Dane	--	--	8	2	--	1	--	48	39	102	21	--
Dodge	15	--	84	10	--	9	--	67	80	48	5	--
Door	86	36	632	172	--	52	--	1,189	915	93	10	--
Fond Du Lac	--	--	8	--	--	--	--	50	42	64	18	--
Green	1	--	6	--	--	--	--	53	16	67	67	--
Green Lake	2	--	13	1	--	1	--	23	22	115	17	--
Jefferson	--	--	--	--	--	--	--	5	4	4	2	--
Kenosha	--	--	2	--	--	--	--	5	5	1	105	1
Kewaunee	8	19	121	65	--	5	--	500	300	9	1	--
Manitowoc	2	5	56	12	--	1	--	317	227	146	56	--
Outagamie	56	21	349	115	4	46	7	1,172	762	661	76	--
Ozaukee	--	2	12	9	--	--	--	62	35	25	18	--
Rock	--	--	5	--	--	--	--	29	25	25	10	--
Sheboygan	3	1	21	2	2	--	--	86	57	18	5	--
Walworth	--	--	--	--	--	--	--	--	--	--	--	--
Washington	2	8	47	27	1	1	--	196	122	92	3	--
Waukesha	1	3	17	10	--	--	--	81	47	33	--	--
Winnebago	6	--	61	5	--	4	--	172	155	124	47	--
Total	220	99	1,768	505	7	164	14	4,824	3,478	1,932	546	1
State total	82,094	14,215	281,895	33,981	558	22,044	1,050	479,502	430,805	169,981	36,695	9,312

[1] Includes only those counties that supplied pulpwood in 2005.

All table cells without observations in the inventory sample are indicated by --. Table value of 0 indicates the volume rounds to less than 1 standard cord, unpeeled. Columns and rows may not add to their totals due to rounding.

Table 10.—Number of industrial pulp or particleboard plants in the Lake States,
by product form, species group used, and state, 2005

Product form and species group	Total Lake States	State		
		Michigan	Minnesota	Wisconsin
Roundwood				
Softwoods				
Northern white-cedar	2	2	0	0
Balsam fir	19	3	10	6
Hemlock	4	1	0	3
Jack pine	16	4	7	5
Red pine	15	4	6	5
White pine	13	3	5	5
Spruce	16	2	8	6
Tamarack	10	1	5	4
Other softwoods	3	1	2	0
Total plants using softwoods [1]	23	4	12	7
Hardwoods				
Ash	23	7	6	10
Aspen	35	11	13	11
Balsam poplar	16	6	8	2
Basswood	24	10	9	5
Beech	10	6	0	4
White birch	28	8	10	10
Yellow birch	11	6	0	5
Cottonwood	2	0	1	1
Elm	8	3	1	4
Hickory	2	1	0	1
Hard maple	24	9	3	12
Soft maple	27	10	7	10
Red oak	15	8	1	6
White oak	11	4	1	6
Other hardwoods	8	5	1	2
Total plants using hardwoods [1]	41	12	13	16
Total plants using roundwood [1]	42	12	14	16
Residues				
Softwood	11	2	3	6
Hardwood	20	8	4	8
Total plants using residues [1]	21	8	4	9
Total plants [1]	44	12	14	18

[1] Some plants use more than one species, so numbers in columns are not additive.

Table 11.—Average daily production of active wood-pulp mills in the Lake States, by state, company, location, and type of pulp produced, 2005

(In tons per 24 hours)

Company	Location	Average daily production	Type of pulp produced					
			Sulfite	Kraft	Kraft groundwood	Groundwood/ mechanical	Semi-chemical	Thermo-mechanical
MICHIGAN								
Decorative Panels International, Inc.	Alpena	250	--	--	--	250	--	--
International Paper Co.	Quinnesec	1,257	--	1,257	--	--	--	--
Menasha Packaging Co. LLC	Otsego	220	--	--	--	--	220	--
New Page Corp.	Escanaba	1,348	--	--	1,348	--	--	--
Packaging Corp. Of America	Filer City	361	--	--	--	--	361	--
Sappi Fine Paper	Muskegon	344	--	344	--	--	--	--
Smurfit-Stone Container Corp.	Ontonagon	751	--	--	--	--	800	--
Total		4,531	--	1,601	1,348	250	1,381	--
MINNESOTA								
Boise White Paper, LLC.	International Falls	1,150	--	1,150	--	--	--	--
Certainteed Corp.	Shakopee	310	--	--	--	310	--	--
Georgia-Pacific Corp.	Duluth	220	--	--	--	--	--	220
International Bildrite, Inc.	International Falls	100	--	--	--	100	--	--
International Paper Co.	Sartell	423	--	--	--	--	--	423
Sapppi, LLC	Cloquet	1,211	--	1,211	--	--	--	--
Stora Enso North America	Proctor	325	--	--	--	325	--	--
UPM - Blandin	Grand Rapids	450	--	--	--	450	--	--
Total		4,189	--	2,361	--	1,185	--	643
WISCONSIN								
Domtar Industries, Inc.	Nekoosa	495	--	495	--	--	--	--
Domtar Industries, Inc.	Port Edwards	255	255	--	--	--	--	--
Georgia-Paicfic Corp.	Phillips	90	--	--	--	90	--	--
Mule-Hide Manufacturing	Cornell	130	--	--	--	--	--	130
Packaging Corp. Of America	Tomahawk	1,350	--	--	--	--	1,350	--
Smart Papers, LLC	Park Falls	170	170	--	--	--	--	--
Stora Enso North America	Biron	400	--	--	--	--	--	400
Stora Enso North America	Niagara	250	--	--	--	250	--	--
Stora Enso North America	Stevens Point	200	--	--	--	--	--	200
Stora Enso North America	Wisconsin Rapids	1,200	--	1,200	--	--	--	--
Thilmany, LLC	Kaukauna	420	--	420	--	--	--	--
Wausau Mosinee Paper	Mosinee	212	--	212	--	--	--	--
Wausau Paper	Brokaw	222	222	--	--	--	--	--
Weyerhaeuser Co.	Rothschild	160	160	--	--	--	--	--
Total		5,554	807	2,327	--	340	1,350	730
Lake States total		14,274	807	6,289	1,348	1,775	2,731	1,373

All table cells without observations in the inventory sample are indicated by --.

Table 12.—Annual production of active particleboard and panel mills in the Lake States, by state, company, location, and product produced, 2005

(In million square feet 3/4-inch basis)

Company	Location	Product produced	Annual production
MICHIGAN			
GFP Strandwood Corp.	Hancock	Molded oriented strand board	2
Georgia-Pacific Corp.	Gaylord	Particleboard	200
Louisiana-Pacific Corp.	Newberry	Oriented strand board	72
Louisiana-Pacific Corp.	Sagola	Oriented strand board	201
Weyerhaeuser Co.	Grayling	Oriented strand board	250
		Total	725
MINNESOTA			
Ainsworth Engineered (USA), LLC	Bemidji	Oriented strand board	265
Ainsworth Engineered (USA), LLC	Cook	Oriented strand board	207
Ainsworth Engineered (USA), LLC	Grand Rapids	Oriented strand board	167
Louisiana-Pacific Corp.	Two Harbors	Oriented strand board	67
Norbord Minnesota	Solway	Oriented strand board	219
Trus Joist - Weyerhaeuser	Deerwood	Engineered wood product	n/a
		Total	925
WISCONSIN			
Louisiana-Pacific Corp.	Hayward	Oriented strand board	250
Louisiana-Pacific Corp.	Tomahawk	Oriented strand board	99
Marshfield Doorsystems	Marshfield	Particleboard	79
Rodman Industries	Marinette	Particleboard	7
		Total	435
		Lake States total	2,085

Table 13.—Production and imports of pulpwood, Central States, 2005

(In standard cords, unpeeled)

Product form, species group, and destination	Production by state[1]					Imports			Total receipts
	Illinois	Indiana	Iowa	Missouri	Regional total	Lake States	Other U.S.	Total imports	
Roundwood									
Softwoods									
Lake States	16	--	--	--	16	--	--	--	--
Northeastern States	--	3,750	--	--	3,750	--	--	--	--
Southern States	1,650	--	--	144	1,795	--	--	--	--
Total	1,666	3,750	--	144	5,560	--	--	--	--
Soft hardwoods[2]									
Central States	1,941	6,469	--	1,169	9,579	--	--	--	9,579
Northeastern States	7	514	--	--	522	--	--	--	--
Southern States	4,416	3,759	--	5,513	13,688	--	--	--	--
Total	6,364	10,743	--	6,681	23,788	--	--	--	9,579
Hard hardwoods[3]									
Central States	2,825	9,415	--	242	12,482	--	--	--	12,482
Northeastern States	5	1,723	--	--	1,728	--	--	--	--
Southern States	7,766	5,070	--	77,742	90,578	--	--	--	--
Total	10,596	16,208	--	77,984	104,788	--	--	--	12,482
Total all roundwood									
Central States	4,766	15,884	--	1,411	22,061	--	--	--	22,061
Lake States	16	--	--	--	16	--	--	--	--
Northeastern States	12	5,987	--	--	5,999	--	--	--	--
Southern States	13,832	8,830	--	83,399	106,060	--	--	--	--
Total	18,626	30,701	--	84,810	134,136	--	--	--	22,061
Residues									
Softwoods									
Central States	--	--	4,800	--	4,800	19,320	--	19,320	24,120
Lake States	--	34,248	--	--	34,248	--	--	--	--
Northeastern States	--	665	--	--	665	--	--	--	--
Total	--	34,913	4,800	--	39,713	19,320	--	19,320	24,120
Hardwoods									
Central States	3,952	38,059	13,031	12,382	67,424	5,952	--	5,952	73,376
Lake States	--	3,838	1,695	--	5,533	--	--	--	--
Northeastern States	--	7,990	--	--	7,990	--	--	--	--
Southern States	9,419	74,423	--	133,428	217,269	--	--	--	--
Total	13,371	124,310	14,725	145,810	298,216	5,952	--	5,952	73,376

(Table 13 continued on next page)

(Table 13 continued)

Product form, species group, and destination	Production by state[1]					Imports			Total receipts
	Illinois	Indiana	Iowa	Missouri	Regional total	Lake States	Other U.S.	Total imports	
Total all residues									
Central States	3,952	38,059	17,831	12,382	72,224	25,272	--	25,272	97,496
Lake States	--	38,086	1,695	--	39,781	--	--	--	--
Northeastern States	--	8,655	--	--	8,655	--	--	--	--
Southern States	9,419	74,423	--	133,428	217,269	--	--	--	--
Total	13,371	159,223	19,525	145,810	337,929	25,272	--	25,272	97,496
Total all wood material									
Central States	8,718	53,943	17,831	13,793	94,285	25,272	--	25,272	119,557
Lake States	16	38,086	1,695	--	39,797	--	--	--	--
Northeastern States	12	14,643	--	--	14,655	--	--	--	--
Southern States	23,251	83,252	--	216,826	323,329	--	--	--	--
Total	31,997	189,924	19,525	230,619	472,065	25,272	--	25,272	119,557

[1] Includes amount of roundwood cut or residues generated by each state.
[2] Hardwood species with an average specific gravity of 0.50 or less.
[3] Hardwood species with an average specific gravity greater than 0.50.
All table cells without observations in the inventory sample are indicated by -- .
Columns and rows may not add to their totals due to rounding.

Table 14.—Central States pulpwood production, by product form and species group, 2001-05

(In standard cords, unpeeled)

Product form and species group	2001	2002	2003	2004	2005
Roundwood					
Softwoods	2,110	3,432	5,485	3,854	5,560
Soft hardwoods[1]	50,939	25,783	31,393	30,363	23,788
Hard hardwoods[2]	113,062	121,600	113,501	131,934	104,788
Total	166,111	150,815	150,380	166,151	134,136
Residues					
Softwood	117	1,860	1,860	1,071	39,713
Hardwood	302,510	274,219	310,161	316,767	298,216
Total	302,627	276,079	312,021	317,838	337,929
Total all wood material	468,738	426,895	462,400	483,989	472,065

[1] Hardwood species with an average specific gravity of 0.50 or less.

[2] Hardwood species with an average specific gravity greater than 0.50.

Columns may not add to their totals due to rounding.

Table 15.—Central States pulpwood production, by state and destination, 2001-05

(In thousand standard cords, unpeeled)

Year	Illinois			Indiana			Iowa			Missouri		
		Destination			Destination			Destination			Destination	
	Total	Central States	Other States	Total	Central States	Other States	Total	Central States	Other States	Total	Central States	Other States
2001	75	22	53	160	67	93	44	43	1	190	14	175
2002	59	9	50	135	54	82	30	29	1	202	14	188
2003	44	10	35	154	53	101	25	23	2	239	19	221
2004	38	10	28	159	57	102	25	23	2	262	19	243
2005	32	9	23	190	54	136	20	18	2	231	14	217
5-year average	50	12	38	160	57	103	29	27	2	225	16	209

Columns may not add to their totals due to rounding.

Table 16.—Average daily production of active wood-pulp mills in the Central States, by company, location, and type of pulp produced, 2005

(In tons per 24 hours)

Company	Location	Average daily production	Type of pulp produced	
			Groundwood/ mechanical	Semi-chemical
International Paper Co.	Terre Haute, Indiana	250	--	250
International Paper Co.	Fort Madison, Iowa	80	--	80
Jeld-Wen Fiber Of Iowa	Dubuque, Iowa	76	76	--
Huebert Fiberboard, Inc.	Boonville, Missouri	80	80	--
	Total	486	156	330

All table cells without observations in the inventory sample are indicated by -- .